PSYCHOLOGY, MORALITY AND EDUCATION

PSYCHOLOGY, MORALITY AND EDUCATION

Edited and Introduced by

The Very Reverend Canon

FERNAND VAN STEENBERGHEN

Professor at the University of Louvain

TEMPLEGATE

SPRINGFIELD, ILLINOIS

This translation from the original French, Psychologie et Pastorale (Études de Pastorale 6, Paris, Desclée de Brouwer; Louvain, É. Nauwelaerts), was made by

RUTH MARY BETHELL

NIHIL OBSTAT: JOANNES M. T. BARTON, S.T.D., L.S.S.
CENSOR DEPVTATVS
IMPRIMATVR: ✠ GEORGIVS L. CRAVEN
EPISCOPVS SEBASTOPOLIS
VICARIVS GENERALIS
WESTMONASTERII: DIE XII MAII MCMLVIII

PRINTED IN GREAT BRITAIN

CONTENTS

INTRODUCTION

By Canon Fernand Van Steenberghen

Professor at the University of Louvain

THIS volume is the outcome of discussions among Belgian priests which took place at Dalhem in the diocese of Liège in 1951. About forty priests were there, and the theme was, the bearing of contemporary psychology on pastoral work. It was an inspiring theme and the papers read were of a high standard, often provoking very fruitful exchanges of views.

The six published here are those which seem most likely to be of interest to a wider circle of readers.

The first elaborates the main theme of the talks. Canon J. Nuttin, who is already known to a number of priests through his important work, *Psychanalyse et conception spiritualiste de l'homme* (Louvain, 1951), was invited to preside over the discussions, and his contribution, serving as introduction to our book, makes a striking case for the importance of psychology for priests who desire their ministry to be as effective as possible.

Next come two studies of general interest, fundamental in character. Readers will appreciate the shrewdness and penetration of Canon H. Widart on *freedom* and Canon J. Vieujean on *responsibility* and *the sense of sin*.

The last three papers deal with specific subjects; they, too, are significant. One is, *the influence of psychology on aspects of education*; another, *the part psychology may play in the discernment of a vocation*; and the last, *the importance of psychology to the whole problem of prayer*.

These topics are dealt with by priests whose competence is known: Abbé L. Fourneau, philosopher and teacher, for many years Inspector of Primary Education; Abbé L. Évely, with his valuable experience in the training and guidance of young people; and Canon D. Joos, the greatly revered former spiritual director of the Bonne-Espérance Seminary.

It is impossible in so short a space to mention all the stimulating ideas that emerged during the Dalhem discussions. But we may take our clue from Canon Nuttin's closing talk and summarize as follows:

All present gained a clearer understanding of how in the light of contemporary psychology the diverse aspects of human life (education, sex, vocation, prayer, etc.) have their own place in the much wider context of the total personality and its environment. Once we admit this, we obtain insight into the whole interplay of relations and influences in which all the different elements of a personality are involved; and the priest is put on his guard against a too narrow, unilateral interpretation of moral problems.

The capital part played by human relations in a priest's pastoral activities was never lost to sight during any of our sessions. We came to the conclusion that all too often a priest's influence is impaired by a certain caste feeling causing him to be ill-at-ease in social environments other than those he knows best; and further, that many priests whose education and teaching experience have accustomed them to mix freely with young people feel awkward and out of place in the adult lay world; a "technique of conversation" for use in the various situations in which a priest may find himself in the course of his duties might be worth considering! Indeed, social psychology, which studies human relations as such, could certainly help to make contacts between priests and laity much more beneficial and fruitful.

A priest as director of consciences and moral counsellor often has to come to grips with the psychological difficulties that people meet with in the conduct of their moral life. The

Dalhem talks underlined the relevance of depth psychology for the understanding and treatment of such difficulties, which are liable to have roots in the distant past, in experiences belonging to early infancy or adolescence which it is important to bring to light. And there are numbers of moral imperfections that should also be considered as psychological deficiencies in the development of a personality.

On the other hand, the priest needs to be on his guard against a possible abuse of psychological methods in pastoral work: we may never look upon the people we are directing as interesting "cases" to "observe"; nor may we treat them as though we were ourselves "psychologists". Any notions of psychology we may acquire have to be placed at the service of a ministry which of its very nature must remain human and priestly, and be firmly established on a basis of commonsense and genuine supernatural charity.

I

PSYCHOLOGY FOR PRIESTS

By Canon Joseph Nuttin

Professor at the University of Louvain

IN the following article, serving as introduction to this book of essays, we discuss how far contemporary psychology could be useful to priests and help them to solve certain problems relating to pastoral work. But first let us formulate some of the problems which today preoccupy the clergy.

I. THE PROBLEMS

A priest's vocation and training

To begin with *vocation*. Apart from the theological and canonical questions that arise, a vocation has certain psychological aspects that deserve our attention with a view to improving methods of recruitment. For the future priest's own happiness as well as the dignity of the priesthood, unfavourable psychological factors and evidence of unsuitability should be detected, as far as possible, at an early stage. Such a vetting can but stress our care not to overlook indications furnished by the Author of human nature Himself. Certain methods of psychological diagnosis might well be studied and adapted to this end.

Present-day society being what it is, full of tensions and conflicts of a moral order, there is in the population at large a growing danger of psychic disequilibrium from which the priest himself is not necessarily immune. To represent intellectual and moral values in a society that questions them, and stand up for them in public, demands spiritual equilibrium and integration of a high quality, such as was not required of a man figuring as a symbol of religious values in a society more than half-willing to accept them. A personality with little stability, bred and nurtured in a hot-house atmosphere, is liable to be perturbed on coming into contact with a civilization rent and torn as ours is. It means that special vigilance is imperative, and some of the methods preconized by science are not to be despised. Cardinal Tisserand said so not long ago, in a remarkable discussion on contemporary psychology in relation to the priesthood: "Recent developments in psychology and the social sciences bring a priest face to face with things he is not accustomed to, but that is no excuse for thinking he may ignore them."

Then there are noticeable gaps in the *training* of priests. As a rule a very minor place is allotted to the positive study of human conduct, i.e. psychology. We have the impression that the apostolate would benefit if more intensive training in psychology were available. Cardinal Tisserand stresses this point too, declaring that a priest engaged in apostolic work has no right to profess ignorance of psychology and the social sciences. And indeed, though endowed with supernatural illumination and powers, theology itself, he says, is in duty bound to seek the support of those sciences in its endeavour to find ever more satisfactory ways of bringing men to God.

In several training centres the syllabus of studies in the subjects Cardinal Tisserand mentions is actually undergoing revision. For instance, in the *écoles sociales* which prepare their students for social work in industry they make "human relations" the basis of any assistance given in a professional capacity. These schools offer specially planned courses in psychology and foster the formation of study groups and discussion classes.

The question would seem to be of equal importance in

training for the priesthood. An intensive course in the psychology of human relations could be of great assistance to a priest in his future work, and it is a fact that studies in social psychology have largely concentrated on this field during recent years.

In addition, priests should know more about the affective life and the complexity of motivation, which in different forms rule people's conduct all through the successive stages of human life. They should be able to grasp the deep-seated emotive forces that underlie certain difficulties of development and behaviour in the child, and also certain of the mechanisms that lead to disturbances in adult conduct. Trends in contemporary psychology throw light on various aspects of these problems, and these new views complement the over intellectual concepts of our traditional psychology. For the priest's standard training prepares him to treat people first and foremost as *minds*, even when he is trying to help them tackle their difficulties and "faults". Now mind is of the greatest importance and is undoubtedly not to be neglected, but other factors are also present. As Cardinal Tisserand goes on to say, "It is a grave mistake to treat people as though they were merely minds. The emotive forces of nature, physical and animal, must not be forgotten, so often driving them blindly in contrary directions".

Whereas those engaged in directing people towards less exalted ends often apply themselves to an intensive study of these problems, the priest usually has to be content—on the human plane—with the wisdom and good sense transmitted by a tradition which is in itself beyond all praise. But we wonder whether it would not be wise to supplement this wisdom and good sense with a little basic science. By which we mean not only philosophical psychology and some notion of experimental psychology—it might even be opportune to introduce a course on the *psychology of human conduct*, studying both its dynamic depths and its external forms. But that is impossible until a specialist in the subject can be appointed to the teaching staff of every greater seminary. He should be as indispensable there as the specialist in canon law or liturgy.

Training in theory alone is, however, insufficient. The priestly apostolate demands great maturity and a profound understanding of people in all the varied and difficult situations of their lives. That part of a psychology course cannot be learnt from books. In some countries, seminarists and young priests are now given practical experience by means of probationary periods in hospitals, schools and institutions, parishes, etc., under the direction of priests specially trained for the purpose. Properly speaking, this is not only practice-work in the field of human relations, but real pastoral work too. In some countries, if conveniently timed, military service could provide a wonderful opportunity for training of this type, always supposing a number of young priests available (and it would mean some years of preparation) to organize and work it, in small groups. At all events, we commend the probation method, in the forms in which it is already being tried out elsewhere, to your serious attention. Indeed, practical work under supervision is a type of training that has proved worth while in all sorts of enterprises, and we are left wondering whether there is anyone who would be more likely to benefit by it than the priest-trainee himself.

The future priest also needs to get rid of his own complexes and psychic difficulties. As he goes about his work, pastoral or educational as it may be, his reactions may now and again be too purely subjective, owing to internal conflicts and complexes of which he probably has no idea. This is liable to occur particularly in educational work. So appropriate training, theoretical and practical, might prove most helpful as a supplement to the spiritual direction he already receives.

Finally, a more psychological attitude in the average theo-

logian would serve to stimulate a revival of interest in several
of the branches of study proposed for the perusal of the priest-
trainee. We have in mind not only ascetical theology and
ethics, where the need is all too evident, but also certain
aspects of dogmatic theology itself. Take for instance the
treatise, *De virtute religionis*: normally the seminarist hopes
to derive great benefit from it, he expects to find illumination
on that major mystery of man, that supremely problematical
side of him, that crops up under the heading of "religion".
After all, a priest's life is going to be focused on the religious
aspect of the human personality, and he wants help in understanding something of the psychological reality that religion
is. Yet, sad to say, he is all too often bitterly disappointed.
Philosophers, and psychologists, and sociologists, all have important things, or at least interesting things to say about
religious feeling and the religious point of view, but our
treatise appears to be unaware of it; if it has retained a few
abstract formulas, it is only with a view to systematic refuta-
tion. Sometimes all it does is to state that such and such concepts are incomplete or inexact; preferring to dwell on the
casuistry of sabbatical observance and similar themes.

This is only one example, and we need not exaggerate the
implications. But it does show how absence of any psychological or sociological orientation, as understood by Cardinal
Tisserand, can have a very regrettable effect on the training
of the clergy. The theoretical material put before them fails
to make impact, because religious phenomena are not situated
in their *human reality* and studied there.

This brings us to a reflection of a more general nature.

It is no secret that in our day the Catholic religion and
Catholic philosophy are on the defensive, on account of the
subjective and psychological attitude of the modern mental
sciences. Too frequently the essential values, truth and goodness, are taken as mere expressions of psychological or social

dispositions; their character as transcendent and eternal values tends to vanish. Our resentment and antagonism are justified, because wherever psychology impinges on philosophy and religion, it is the *objective* character of these values that we like to stress—and indeed it is essential to do so.

But it is not desirable that a traumatic experience of modernism should continue to fixate our defensive reaction. We must recognize that a subjective or psychological component is present in any concept, any activity or human reality (whether religion, philosophy, ethics, science, or art) and has to be taken into account; to do so is indeed the very condition of grasping the things of the spirit at all adequately.

One regrettable result of our neglect is our own tendency to present the eternal values in forms that are, psychologically and humanly speaking, out-of-date. By neglecting psychology, we perpetuate antiquated formulas and attempt to generalize and impose on others a very specialized psychological attitude—our own. It is distressing how whole branches of study of special concern to us—e.g. religious psychology—went ahead without us, and often against us. It is time we abandoned our distrustful, defensive attitude—though without exaggerating and running into the opposite danger. The gain in clarity on the human side of our studies, theological and philosophical, would be enormous, and our training would come so much closer to real life—the future priest's own life no less than that of his future flock.

Spiritual guidance and education

We mentioned the psychology of human relations: many of the problems of pastoral psychology are different aspects of this theme. We will consider two of them, under the headings of "spiritual guidance", and "education of the young".

As regards the former we have in mind confession, the formation of a child's conscience, the guidance of adolescent boys and girls, that of adults in sometimes difficult, complicated situations, that of souls in distress, of unbalanced consciences, and finally, talks with the sick and old. All these are so many forms of human relations. The question is, whether there is anything to add or improve in the methods transmitted by tradition, full of human wisdom and supernatural inspiration as they are. As it happens, young priests, more often than not, are totally ignorant of them. Now young priests ought to know how and in what circumstances these various forms of human relations can be established, for as a rule they mostly fail to materialize at all.

To turn to education. Everyone knows and appreciates the admirable degree of devotion that is evident in all departments of education, whether that of normal or handicapped children, on the part of religious and on the part of the secular clergy. But in education as elsewhere, devotion has to be leavened with competence to be fully effective. At one time, Christian education was "progressive", alive with experiment and improved methods. Today it is almost necessary to impose minimum standards. In some countries, though all too seldom, Catholic education authorities are keen to establish psychological and educational research centres, and that implies that there are people eager to discover the best methods for school orientation and for dealing with the difficulties in psychic development and adaptation that occur among school children. Whereas in other countries no one shows any interest at all. Ignorance has a knack of making complicated things look quite easy. No harm would be done if we were to revise our own views from time to time. For it is useless to take refuge in the fact that our *principles* and *intentions* are above reproach. In the field of education and re-education, it is the spirit of initiative that must not be allowed to die down. We keep on saying how much we mind about education, quite rightly too, but we also need to remember that in our day progress in method occurs largely with the help of scientific research. To take an example, our schools are far from exhausting the means at their disposal for dealing with backward and difficult children, of which every classroom has its quota. All too often, the only steps taken aim at preventing them from doing any harm. They go on from the bottom of one class to the bottom of the next without anyone to take up their case authoritatively. And we must not forget that a country needs a long tradition of organized practice and research in this field before any results worth mentioning can be apparent.

Those are a few of the problems. There are many more. But we wanted to stress the more urgent ones.

II. CONTEMPORARY PSYCHOLOGY

Difficult applications

After our brief survey of problems, let us now see if contemporary psychology can throw any light on them, and whether or no it can propose solutions.

In some countries, but certainly not everywhere, there is a tendency to overestimate the possible relevance of psychology to the field of pastoral work. The chief reason for not expecting too much from it, or at least not in the immediate future, is that this science has developed, so far, without our concurrence, and indeed often in a hostile spirit. Psychology, as it is today, presupposes a conception of man largely opposed to our own. Even worse, its views, methods and so-called "results" are often inextricably mingled with theoretical elements which make their immediate application very difficult for us. That is specially so as regards depth psychology. So there is no hope of simply taking advantage of what others have accomplished. We shall have to pay a high price for our passive attitude and lack of interest hitherto. And as we said just now, tangible results are unlikely till long and laborious preparatory work has been done, and this means groups of dedicated workers and periods of exploration and experiment. Now nothing is more harmful than the amateur spirit in this field. It happens all too frequently that a well-intentioned priest wants to take his ignorance in hand and thinks his lack of training in psychology can be remedied by reading something. Then we have the embarrassing experience of being asked to recommend a "good book" that will give him all the knowledge and training needed. It is an impossible request: no key to the problem is to be found in any one book. Besides, it is not a question of keys but of a steady effort to improve methods, however slightly. And that aim is sufficiently worth while for us to take advantage of any technical advances that occur, if they are conducive to a better understanding of human conduct. What we need for the moment is not simple applications of psychology to our problems; and what is lacking is not priests who are "interested in psychology"; but first and foremost, and for long years ahead, we need trained professional men from among existing and future priests; a handful of specialists charged to do research work on the problems of psychology wherever they impinge on the field of pastoral activities—all over the world. Qualified men who would also be able to adapt their teaching methods to the needs of future priests, helping them to prepare for the concrete tasks ahead of them.

By this means, the advances of modern psychology could gradually accrue to pastoral activities in the manner best befitting conditions in any given country or community. For we must never forget that methods which may prove excellent elsewhere are not necessarily the right ones to apply here.

Now let us consider what is *new* in present-day psychology, and how it may modify the bearing of psychology on pastoral work.

Psychology is, of course, no longer that part of the philosophy course in which the vegetative and sensitive life or the faculties of the soul are dealt with. Nor is it merely an accumulation of experimental data relating to sensation, memory, and time series, as given in older works on experimental psychology. We all know how bitterly disappointing that type of psychology proved to be for those who turned to it in the hope of consolidating their knowledge and comprehension of man.

There are three main currents of modern psychology to be mentioned as affecting its practical bearing, and as being applicable to one or another form of pastoral work. These are: dynamic psychology, called *depth psychology; experimental psychology*, with its methods of diagnosis of the personality and aptitudes; and finally, *social psychology*. We will take each in turn.

Depth psychology and psycho-analysis

Depth psychology has put us into contact with the accumulated content of psychic life. Indeed, to know and understand man implies some contact with this accumulated content. Formerly, of course, scientific psychology did not go beyond an examination of psychic processes functioning in a vacuum as it were. The abundant material and the interest of "clinical" psychology, as opposed to "laboratory" psychology, are due precisely to the way it establishes contact with accumulated experience, that is to say, with *what* a person thinks, imagines, desires, and so on; and attempts to make us *understand*. For the special character of a psychic phenomenon must not be forgotten: in so far as it is a process it can be *observed* experimentally like any other phenomenon; but in that it is accumulated experience—which is a character proper to it—it can be understood. Scientific psychology used to approach this accumulated content with great distrust, due to unfortunate earlier experiences with the introspective method. But thanks to its clinical experience, contemporary psychology has now embarked on a new line of approach to that psychic content and all its affective tensions and underlying mechanisms—and a most rewarding line it has proved to be. It has succeeded in making us comprehend that content, in its genesis and above all in the complex mechanism of its affections and tensions.

Obviously, this whole range of studies is very important for anyone who has to understand and guide human conduct. Knowing and understanding man consists above all in unravelling the content of his dynamic and affective life, that is to say, understanding the motives, intentions and forces that induce his behaviour or inhibit it. Laboratory psychology had not been able to throw much light on all this. It had chiefly studied the psychological repercussions of the affections and emotions. Whereas traditional psychology merely drew up its rational diagrams of motivation and human behaviour. On that basis our standard psychology still attempts to influence and direct the "reasonable" being who is man. But today, thanks to depth psychology, we know from the evidence how much more complicated human conduct and its motivation are. And above all, we now know the approaches to a comprehension of all sorts of irrational conduct and affections; here the traditional method had no clue, though these matters are often the object of spiritual guidance, or education, or re-education.

Now we may enquire more positively, what *is* the contribution of depth psychology?

From the theoretical standpoint, what chiefly extended our comprehension of human conduct was the discovery of the genetic relation that exists between certain affective conflicts of infantile life, and given tendencies, given traits of character, given conceptions, attractions and aversions, and ways of behaving, in the life of an individual; the discovery of the actual processes by which the accumulated experiences of the past engendered and continue to influence present conduct; allowing us the better to comprehend the idiosyncrasies and difficulties of character that we come across, and the tendencies and general behaviour connected with them.

From the practical point of view, this better comprehension furnishes us with new therapeutic methods. This means that we have a greater variety of means at our disposal for putting people on the right road and helping them to keep to it. For instance—and this is an important point—it can now be proved that certain faults are deficiencies in a personality's development which have to be treated, and if possible cured, and not vices to be combated without more ado. We cannot linger on this point, but let us remark in passing that this type of psychology, elaborated by Freud and supplemented by a number of different authors, contains elements that are extremely valuable for the priest. It can moreover contribute to that catharsis by which the future priest will rid himself of his personal difficulties and internal conflicts, and will be a useful complement to training in education and the direction of consciences.

Yet one thing must be stressed: although of such great importance for the priest, this particular psychological trend is the most treacherous of all in its effects on pastoral work in the present-day world. It is a form of psychology that has developed without us, as we remarked earlier. The clergy were behindhand in admitting its importance. Moreover it contains very serious omissions—hence dangers—which must not be overlooked. To counter them the priest will have to be well aware of them, and that is why we should devote some minutes to the subject now.

Omissions and dangers in depth psychology

What is the nature of these omissions and dangers in depth psychology, and more particularly in psycho-analysis?

Sigmund Freud, the founder of the system, himself admitted that psycho-analysis was only concerned with one section of psychic activity, the unconscious part of it. Thus, said Freud, psycho-analysis will never be able to provide more than partial solutions. But this critical view of the limited bearing of psycho-analytical data was quickly forgotten, by the founder of the system himself, and above all by many of his disciples. So what is but one aspect or one element of psychic activity has come to be taken for the whole of it. Thus, even the positive and precise data of psycho-analysis often tend to falsify the true picture of man's psychic life, simply because these data have been separated from the overall framework in which they should in fact be considered. While doing very significant work from the scientific point of view, disclosing facts and mechanisms hitherto unknown, many psycho-analysts offend our view of man in the round, giving a wrong idea of the complete picture, taking the part for the whole. The complexity of human activity has been reduced to one of its elements. That is a first omission and a first danger.

An immediate remedy is not to be found simply in teaching the Christian conception of man. Such a serious error of perspective in the description of positive facts must be put right on the level of the science itself. It derives mainly from the fact that psycho-analysis evolved in a vacuum, ignorant of and ignoring the general psychology of man; but it also derives from the fact that our traditional psychology did not know how to use and integrate the new discoveries that were being made. So we have to put the facts and mechanisms discovered by Freud back into their right place in the total picture of man as we know him, and thus bring into existence a more balanced and a *truer* psychology of the human personality. We believe it is very important not to try to correct mistakes made at the theoretical stage, or on the level of scientific interpretation, by an application of purely philosophical and religious principles; for by using methods of that kind we risk creating the impression that our Christian conception of man is in conflict with science, and then situations arise that can only be deplored.

Indeed, there is more to it than that; for beside the facts and mechanisms that psycho-analysis has discovered, with more or less certainty or probability, there exists a whole philosophy of man and human culture as developed by Freud and some of his disciples. It consists of views that overstep by a long mark the bounds of a sane scientific theory verifiable by reference to facts, and the result is merely a bad human philosophy. These views are the product of reasonings based often on vague analogies between "higher" and "lower" psychic activities, or hasty generalizations from the unconscious and instinctive elements entering into the composition of an activity. The bad psycho-analytical philosophy is not for an educated man the most dangerous element in psycho-analysis; what is, to our mind, much more serious, is the artificial isolation of facts removed from their true perspective.

Adequately to oppose the philosophy or *Weltanschauung* of psycho-analysis, the Christian conception of man must be adequately presented. It must be presented as a philosophical and religious system containing a total and spiritual view of man in harmony with the whole of the facts.

The points raised so far concern the *theoretical* knowledge of man. There remains to stress an *ethical* factor in the conflict between psycho-analysis and the Christian conception of man.

The most deplorable effect that depth psychology (and psycho-analysis in particular) has had on our contemporaries is in changing their moral attitude to conduct, each man's own and other people's. In company with many other currents of thought in modern life, depth psychology has contributed to diminish a man's sense of responsibility for his own actions; it has paralysed all effort conducive to wholesome self-control and to the constructive expansion of the personality. In certain circumstances it is all too convenient to consider human conduct as dominated by unconscious and instinctive forces. The laying bare of the unconscious has given man the impression that his life evolves inside him without his connivance. Contemporary literature only stresses this view. As a consequence, precious reserves of spiritual forces and values run the risk of remaining unexplored, whether in education or in the growth of the individual. Man's conscious autonomous activity, which was pushed on one side by the *theoretical* conception of man, is here utterly disregarded as a positive factor in the building up of a personality. In education this attitude is calculated to paralyse an important part of the child's constructive powers.

From the specifically Christian point of view, the notion of sin is liable to lose its profound significance in this psychological climate. A badly understood and badly popularized psycho-analytical theory conditions a man to attribute every moral fault to the sole forces of the unconscious or instinct. He stops begging God for forgiveness for his failures and he is unlikely to engage his whole personality in the fight for an ideal. It is the "impersonal" unconscious element in him that he will blame for deviations in his conduct. By shifting its centre of gravity over towards the unconscious, human personality becomes drained of its true meaning and value, consisting as they do of mind and conscience, freedom and responsibility.

All of this, we repeat, has nothing to do with the positive data discovered by psycho-analysis as a valid branch of science. The great error in the moral field which now concerns us comes from the confusion of the normal with the pathological. It is true, in certain unbalanced people there are pathological complexes which correspond to what one is accustomed to call "sin", and the priest should know this and take it into account. It is also true that in these cases what has to be done is to release a morbid conscience from its sense of guilt rather than appeal to the sense of responsibility—another very important fact for directors of consciences. Moreover in these cases it is wiser to counsel psychological relaxation and repose rather than ascetical exercises. But in all such instances we are dealing with pathological states, and that must not be forgotten.

In a normal man, a sustained effort towards an ideal, and the state of psychic tension that results, can achieve great things; but in a dislocated personality they may be agents of destruction. That is the plain truth. It is also the reason why, so often, priest and psycho-therapeutist do not agree. They work along opposite lines, the priest insisting on effort, the therapeutist on relaxation and repose.

So the methods found useful in giving guidance to a normal person may prove harmful in unbalanced and pathological cases. And it is no less true that certain ideas and methods appropriate in psycho-therapy can have a paralysing effect on the education and guidance of normal people. The same may be observed of bodily health: exercises and training profitable for the healthy body may be disastrous for a sick organism; and nothing is more injurious to the physical development of a normal person than certain forms of rest and treatment which may be of great benefit to the sick.

In the moral sphere, another attitude, the one which tends to minimize the part played by conscious and spiritual forces in human conduct, also derives from an illegitimate generalization of psycho-analytical data. Notions relevant to a pathological case tend more and more to be taken as valid for mankind in general. Freudian theory has given great impetus to the trend to confuse the normal and the pathological; and all who are studying depth psychology with a view to educational and pastoral work among normal people, should be forewarned of this danger in the strongest terms. We are well aware that pathological strains are evident in the psychic development of any man, just as microbes are mingled in the air we breathe. But it is essential to know, too, how in a fundamentally well-balanced person certain germs of morbid behaviour are often best cured by action stimulating the normal forces of development, rather than by concentrating on the pathological strain. To adopt this sane attitude towards the psychic conflicts that appear in a normal man, and act accordingly, requires, in combination, a profound knowledge of the pathological and a great love of the normal. Some priests' infatuation for psychological and psycho-analytical studies is such that it engenders and nurtures a predilection for unbalanced and pathological cases. These men are very unsuitable candidates for the study of psychology.

So it is evident that the psychological training of a priest, and the application of contemporary psychology to pastoral work, present problems that cannot be solved merely by "reading a book". Nor can these problems be solved by inaugurating a course of study where modern psychology is brought in as an "extra" to traditional, out-of-date psychology. The task that confronts us is, first, to elaborate a *philosophical* psychology that will account for problems as they emerge from this new perspective of the facts with which we are concerned. Then, to collaborate in developing a *positive* psychology which will scrutinize the totality of "human facts" and respect them, interpreting them within the framework of a scientific theory broad enough to take all factors into account. For the priest specializing in psychology, here is a twofold task, to be carried out alongside the practical business of giving young clergy psychological training.

The need for a philosophical psychology

The first half of the task, the elaboration of a philosophical psychology, deserves very thorough consideration. There are a number of implications involved. It would be an illusion to suppose that we already possess this philosophical psychology and that so-called scientific facts make no real difference, either to our approach to problems or to our solution of them. It is often stated that *commonsense* is all that is needed. We do not agree. Unless the philosophers have been brooding over the facts for a long period of time and studying the theories of positive psychology at leisure, it is improbable that they will be able to use our traditional philosophy as a scaffolding within which to construct a philosophical psychology sufficiently in touch with human problems as they appear to modern minds. To be still more precise, we hold that now certain discoveries in depth psychology have been made, the problem of freedom for instance has to be viewed from a somewhat different angle; and likewise the interrelation of physical and psychic (or moral) elements; the finality of conduct; and the very nature of psychic phenomena. Thus a host of new problems has arisen since the discovery of certain psycho-therapeutic methods and of the possibilities of cybernetics. The philosopher may have the impression that neither the focus of the problem nor the solution to it are essentially altered by these scientific discoveries. A man of science, in direct contact with the new realities, is not necessarily of the same opinion. His view of "human facts" really has changed; and a philosophy must attempt an ultimate explanation of reality as *perceived by us*. You may believe that the human reality that produces philosophical problems for us to solve is solely governed by commonsense; it is an easy enough position to adopt. But is it sound? From certain points of view it is not. The human reality that posits philosophical problems is man *as he exists for us*. And the way man exists for us depends, among other things, on our scientific knowledge of human facts, and on the level of our contacts with other people. If we meet people chiefly on the plane of com-

monsense and cultural relations, our set of problems will be
different, even theoretically, from that of the psychiatrist,
who meets people mainly on the plane of the psycho-patho-
logical clinic. Granted that certain main lines in the traditional
solutions preserve their full value; but their application and
their adjustment to concrete reality, which has to be explained,
may be subject to profound changes. In the past, the philosopher could keep abreast of the problems affecting man as
they arose. But the very high degree of specialization consequent on scientific progress, not only precludes the possibility
of knowing several branches of science really well, but also
prevents the philosopher from being really *au fait*; how do
given problems look to those habitually engaged in studying
man or scrutinizing people from their own particular angle?
It is not absolutely certain that the special shape the problems
take on is entirely the product of their unilateral training.
Their way of seeing human reality does really raise special
problems. And that is the reason why, as a rule, philosophical
psychology treats the philosophical problems concerning man
in the form in which they exist "for the philosopher". But
that, too, is a specialist's viewpoint, or so it seems to us; nor
can it be completely freed of the charge of being unilateral.

At all events—even if we abstract these subjective differences (which are, however, not always void of theoretical
validity)—philosophical problems do arise concerning ways
of being and acting which are essential to man as man. And
anyone who knows what he is talking about, realizes that our
present views on these essential forms of psychical activity can
no longer be based solely on commonsense. Science has discovered facts, and above all, science has attempted to give
scientific explanations, with the result that we are compelled
to see man's psychic activity in a new light. In our opinion, a
philosophy of man must start from a total view, including the
data of commonsense and the data of science, which together

make up the complicated picture of man as he is to be seen by men of our time.

The problem of the relation between positive science and philosophy takes one form for psychology and another for the natural sciences. One of the reasons for this difference is, that the psychic phenomenon essentially implicates the whole of the human personality. A new view of certain factors such as science provides, directly affects our conception of the aggregate personality, much more so than in the case of the physical sciences. In other words, new facts as to the mechanism of human conduct affect our conception of personality, i.e. as involving individual freedom, more directly than discoveries in nuclear physics affect the cosmological problems of change.

Thus depth psychology, and contemporary psychology in general, not only constitute so much new material for the priest to add to his traditional psychology, but a whole new set of problems, only to be solved by an intensive study of human psychology, both on the philosophical plane and on the plane of positive science.

Methods of psychological diagnosis

There is a quite different field of contemporary psychology which might be relevant to pastoral work in certain respects, specially in the orientation and education of young people. It is the study of individual aptitudes and qualities by means of the *test method*. We need only touch on it here, for it is more or less a technical matter. The method is often better known in its abuse than for its basic principles—but it has made great progress in recent years. Competently applied, it can doubtless render good service at all stages of education and be of assistance in orientation and re-education.

In primary and secondary education, as we observed, it can help us to deal with difficult cases; assuming that the tests used have first been standardized and validated, as they have to be.

It is regrettable that pioneer work and progress in this field so seldom come from our own schools and establishments. We are in fact so often preoccupied with the fact of sheer numbers, that other things tend to be submerged—and among them our concern for improving methods and helping our children in the best way possible. Many of the responsibilities we have taken on in the more specialized branches of education and re-education demand a most scrupulous diagnosis of children's personality, traits of character, aptitudes, or psychological deficiencies, as the case may be; for instance in the re-education of juvenile delinquents, the instruction of debilitated or maladjusted children, and so on. As we said before, good will and devotion to the task in hand, excellent in themselves, cannot be substitutes for well-considered and tested methods. Indeed devotion and charity should have the primary effect of inciting us to seek out which are the more effective methods for dealing with given difficulties, even prompting us to create methods when advisable, if those in our charge are really to benefit by them.

Another point to be mentioned in passing, though we should like to stress its importance for all branches of education, is the method known in America as "counselling", that is, psychological guidance. We warmly recommend all priests to read R. P. Curran's *Counselling in Catholic Life and Education.*

Social psychology

Finally, we come to a third trend in contemporary psychology, one deserving all the attention a priest can give it. That is, the present extended scope of social psychology.

Together with clinical psychology, social psychology is the most active branch of contemporary psychology. Its importance is immediately apparent, both for its contribution to a better understanding of human conduct in general, and for its relevance to pastoral psychology. Most of the situations in which our activity, our apostolate, engage us are in fact social situations. For men are far less frequently occupied in reacting to some physical stimulant than in behaving in a certain way towards other people. The study of these human relations—which is the main object of social psychology—is of capital importance to the clergy, and to Catholic action in general. We want to stress one point here.

In our society, a change is in process, or has already taken place, in people's relations to one another, and there are psychological changes going on in the very heart of that community of people we call a parish. Also, subtler but none the less real changes are going on in the relations between priest and laity, between authority and subordinate. Chiefly remarkable is a change of attitude: a change of a psychological order. It sets us major problems and on their solution depends the very possibility of mutual comprehension and fruitful co-operation in days to come. Today social psychology—especially in the form inspired by K. Lewin's "field theory"—has successfully tackled several problems which are clearly within the range of pastoral work. For example, leadership has been studied under different aspects, such as the tensions that arise in a collaborating group, the attitude of authority towards members of a group, the repercussions of that attitude on the group's activities and usefulness and even on the character of its members. All this has been carefully noted and written up. We have our own very various activities involving leadership and collaboration, such as youth work, social action, pastoral work proper, all of which might well draw profit from what has been achieved in this field; down to the Church's hierarchical structure itself. But it is more than likely that the clergy world will be among the last to realize that a new type of human relations is emerging, as in contacts between authority and subject, clergy and laity, and so on. The obstacle to an adaptation is not, after all, evangelical doctrine: more likely it will be our own frame of mind. Sometimes we are taken to task in a general way for our lack of a spirit of collaboration as among equals. Some of the fruits of social psychology might with advantage be applied to *our* problems and *our* various situations, and they would prove to be of great service to us; that is, if we really do want to understand and keep our eyes open.

Those are some of the trends of modern psychology likely to be of increasing interest to the clergy and to pastoral work. We said at the beginning that in its present state this psychology has not much to offer of immediate relevance to our problems. But it has proved it is capable of tackling them and even of throwing an astonishing degree of light on them. Now it is our turn to get down to the job. For our problems must be scrutinized and dealt with according to *our* views, taking into account *our* special situations, and *our conception of man* must also be taken into account.

Our conception of man in relation to psychology is therefore yet another point that merits attention.

Psychology and our conception of man

When psychology merely studied sensations and time series, it had very little to do with a conception of man. Modern psychology is different, as we observed in connection with depth psychology. It has drawn closer to reality and to the content of psychical life, and concentrates principally on the affective and dynamic bases of human kind. Indeed, in tampering with the value and the very nature of human personality, it has come right on to the threshold of our own field.

The value of a personality depends largely on what determines its activity or conduct. If, even on a higher plane, its activity is but a travestied manifestation of an instinctive force

3

and unconscious mechanisms, our picture of man will have to submit to drastic changes.

In our day it is the positive sciences, psychology among them, which most influence our contemporaries' conception of man—quite as much as philosophy. It is psychology that furnished modern literature with the general picture of what it thinks man is like. And it is from psychology that fashionable philosophies have culled many of their favourite features and choicest themes.

Our Christian civilization is very well aware that the spiritual conception of man, its own, is threatened. To counter-act the menace we have fostered Movements. Christian humanism for instance. It is largely by considerations of a philosophical nature, and articles with a literary flavour, that we try to defend the spiritual conception of man.

But demolition is going on from the base upwards; it is done with the assistance of *positive* scientific data. It causes conflicts in the minds of our own scientists, conflicts none the less dangerous for being latent. We attempted elsewhere to describe this conflict between two different conceptions of man, which is the more apparent in university circles:

"In social and cultural daily life, the scientist still adheres to the traditional conception of man. In that setting he still treats the human person as an autonomous being with self-control, occupying an exceptional place in nature. But back in his laboratory he insensibly and unwittingly modifies his mode of thought. There, the human person is simply re-integrated in the impersonal 'becoming' of nature and the system of instinctive forces which constitutes the dynamism of life."

A whole aura surrounds these notions—born of the prestige enjoyed by the positive data on which they are supposed to rest. It is of no use to confront them with purely speculative and "humanist" theories about man. We must produce our own conception of man, one reposing on data and methods of the same type. What we need even more than a philosophical psychology is a coherent system of positive psychology, such that its interpretation of facts, as well as of hypotheses, will do justice to the totality of human personality at all the different levels of its psychic activity.

That is why psychology in the making and psychological theory require the keen interest and active participation of all who are disturbed by the conception of man which our civilization is busy concocting—quite apart from any direct application they may have to pastoral work. And our own performance in general psychology will help to determine what applications may one day be made in the field of religious and pastoral psychology.

In conclusion

Deepen the foundations of our ministry and clarify its psychological aspects: all of us feel it would be opportune to do so. Not as innovation for its own sake, but in order to adapt methods transmitted to us by a tradition rich in human wisdom, and render them more effective still. If our pastoral activity is to correspond to the needs of contemporary men and women, as closely as Christ's and his Apostles' did, we must use present-day aids. Psychology is one of them. Its evolution in recent years brings it right to the brink of things that matter greatly to a priest. But it would be a serious error to suppose that the concepts and methods we need can simply be picked up ready-made. There is even some slight danger of priest-amateurs wanting to improve their pastoral activity by the acquisition of psychological bric-à-brac. One thing alone is essential—a remedy for both ignorance and excess of zeal—it is *for the clergy to have their own specialists.* Just as in any other field that impinges on pastoral work and the apostolate.

What we shall now need is priests with years of intensive

training in psychology behind them. Their job will be to do research work on general pastoral problems and on specific ones, taking all relevant factors into account. They will also have to lecture to future priests and train them in psychology. In given circumstances they will be counsellors; and they will be qualified to take on any practical or experimental projects that authority may wish to put under their charge.

II

REFLECTIONS ON THE NATURE OF
FREE ACTIVITY

By Canon Henri Widart
Professor at St Joseph's Seminary, Malines

AT the core of the Christian life, divinely given grace and human activity proceed in company. The gift of life which God offers man is a fact, an irrevocable acquisition: Our Saviour Christ is risen. It is a gift with no possible second thoughts to it, continuing all down the centuries of human history.

But God is not the sole agent. For Christ founded His Church and entrusted to it the completion of His mission. The divine gift is, normally, to come to men through men. Moreover men have to accept it. Now both the acceptance of the gift and the human collaboration remain precarious: for man is free. As he goes about his work the apostle always has to take the human element into account; first in himself, as the starting-point of his efforts; and at the receiving end too, in his neighbour, for he would have him live more genuinely dependent on God.

When pastoral psychology, for the greater glory of the apostolate, undertakes a scholarly scrutiny of the apostolic life, it is bound to encounter free, voluntary activity. Clearly human agency constitutes a constant element of the apostolate, a central and indestructible one, which no transformation or reform of apostolic technique can eliminate.

Free, voluntary activity is thus a factor that we cannot by-pass in our present discussions.

How shall we begin? Need we run through the proofs for the *existence* of human freedom? There is probably no point in doing so all over again. Nor, apparently, is it of such great importance. It is only incidentally that a priest has to enlarge on it. And even then the difficulties met with concern mainly the *nature* of the free act. That is the clue we shall follow now, dealing in turn with the various elements that compose human activity, and showing how they interpenetrate. As we proceed we shall be able to challenge a number of commonly-held views about freedom that are, in fact, incorrect.

I. HUMAN FREEDOM—INCARNATE FREEDOM

One source of error, perhaps the principal one, is clear ideas, or rather, *too* clear ideas.

For instance, everyone is aware that "freedom" and "necessity" are on opposite sides. Or again, surely only a moment's reflection is needed to perceive that the notion of freedom includes that of "activity", which, as everyone knows, is the opposite of "passivity". So it is easy to grasp that freedom both implies autonomous conduct and reinforces this "autonomy"; which, in its turn, is understood as the negation of "dependence". People often speak of the spiritual character of freedom, which of course is supposed to mean that it has nothing in common with the organic. And attention is drawn to its transcendence in relation to bodily activity, which it is able to control. Thus, the free being can, as he chooses, govern, direct, and overrule bodily activity.

These few aphorisms belong to the stock of commonly-held clear ideas on the subject of freedom. As a rule they are taken as self-evident. And yet, again and again, they lead to false conclusions. They do, no doubt, represent real aspects of freedom. But for reasons of emphasis they are detached and isolated, with the result that what is described as an abstract notion of freedom no longer, alas, agrees with reality.

Let us start with the freedom-necessity pair.

Certainly they are opposite concepts: whatever is free occurs without necessity, and the epithet "free" is not applicable to what is predetermined. Freedom is often defined as primarily the exclusion of necessity, and likewise, necessity implies the negation of freedom. This conceptual incompatibility is not to be denied. No one, not even God, can alter that; much less any philosopher, however perspicacious he may be.

But can a conceptual incompatibility be carried over into real life just as it is? Let us simply observe that different concepts may serve to express one same reality, that is, of course, if it is viewed under different aspects. Wood is certainly not glass; but our windows are made of both wood and glass. Here there is merely juxtaposition, co-presence, because we are dealing with something made. Let us find a better example. A nervous tissue is not a tegumentary tissue nor a bone tissue nor a muscle; which does not prevent them all from being present together in the human body. This analogy has the advantage of revealing the mutually complementary rôle of the different tissues in the body's structure. One cannot exist without the other, and each has its own dynamic, by which it contributes to the development of the whole, and hence of each of the parts. This can even be put to the test by considering the very appearance of the body: its shape cannot be attributed to the skeleton alone, nor to the tegumentary tissues alone, nor to the muscles alone; all these elements—and many others, but this is not an anatomy course—collaborate, each in its own way, to give any human body the look it has. Here there is no simple juxtaposition: where we deal with life, that is insufficient. There is an integration of various elements.

Such similes do at least suggest that freedom and determinism might be found within one and the same activity, in this case human activity. How are we to conceive this supposed co-existence?—Not as a simple juxtaposition of elements, but as integration. We may recall that in human behaviour different elements, some necessary, others free, do mutually sustain and complete one another. The true nature of human freedom is not grasped so long as this much-neglected fact is not clearly seen. We will now examine it more closely.

To begin with, a few words as to those "necessary" factors which accompany our voluntary activity. They are of different kinds. There is nothing surprising in their plurality, it only reflects the diverse aspects of the human being, and it also corresponds to them.

Of these determined factors, a certain number belong to the purely *physical* order. The law of gravity, for instance, holds good all through. It admits of no exception and no free act can deliver me from it. A really high jump can only be done from a springboard. The pilot of a plane or glider can only get his machine off into the air by means of an ingenious exploitation of the laws of gravity. Material things are put together in a certain way, offering such resistance that without the proper tools a man is incapable of getting through a wall.

To turn now to our own reactions, voluntary activity goes hand in hand with biological determinants. Each tendency, each instinct has a definite physiological aspect, with the appropriate muscular and nervous system, mode of excitation, hormonal secretions, energies, which, in their fundamental structure at least, are fixed and invariable. Finally, there are numerous incoercible reactions which are part and parcel of the determinism of the *psychic* life: images, ideas, desires have a driving force of their own, that is to say, they can incite to action and promote action. The rôle of association is certain.

Recently, psychologists have greatly stressed the importance of the unconscious. Here is a factor which, under normal conditions, that is, apart from psycho-analytical treatment, does not appear in full consciousness. Its dynamism, and hence its very existence, are manifest principally by side-tracking them on to the affective field. Then there is the subconscious, and habits, and character, and so on. And finally, we may observe that it is as a rule by indirect means, through the psychic life, that the world at large and social life influence us, creating habits and prejudices in us, inciting what is termed "moral necessity", nurturing our various tendencies, of which the principal ones are, according to many psychologists, the instincts of sympathy and self-defence.

All these determinisms belong to our nature, and constitute its congenital equipment. They compose what Ricœur calls the "non-voluntary" factor.

Rigid laws of necessity govern these mechanisms. Is that a reason for considering them as the foes of our freedom? The question is whether their only effect is to be a brake on our voluntary activity, an impediment and a burden, and whether their whole might is really bent on shackling freedom. If we were to believe current ideas, that is what it would mean. In fact, faced with this non-voluntary factor in human activity, people often tend to deny the very existence of its basic freedom. So it would be useful to understand why, in human activity, this many-faceted non-voluntary factor is not juxtaposed, but integrated to freedom of action.

(1) Far from being smothered by the non-voluntary, voluntary activity presupposes it, and in fact requires it. In man, the voluntary does not exist apart from the non-voluntary, in fact it does not exist at all unless the latter has reached a certain stage of development. We can picture what the connection is by thinking of a tree's relation to the soil. A tree is something

quite different from the soil, but has an absolute need of it; it is planted in it, caught in it, and growing out of it. In the same way, without sacrificing its own properties, the voluntary is rooted in the non-voluntary. Obviously, during the first phase of his existence, man's behaviour consists merely in unconscious, and thus involuntary, acts. And it is only some years later that voluntary conduct emerges, rather like shoots of wheat issuing from the soil in springtime. The soil does not create the seed, it is already there, but buried. And it only emerges after a preparatory ripening of non-voluntary forces.

(2) The reason for this staggering of our growth is nothing mysterious. For the non-voluntary factor does not merely furnish our will with the conditions for its expansion; integration goes further than that: the voluntary only takes shape at all by dint of utilizing the non-voluntary. For the human will is not in the least creative by itself. It could put nothing together if it did not have recourse to the energies contained in the non-voluntary dynamisms. It is from these that it borrows its constructive power and it is their strength that enriches it.

Thus, in the very constitution of the human will we discover a dependent, passive aspect. Voluntary activity does not solely consist in influencing the non-voluntary; it is also, first and foremost, receptive in regard to it.

That is what present-day philosophers try to insist on when they speak of the "incarnation" of the will, the "incarnation" of freedom. Freedom is, of course, spiritual, but its spirituality does not turn it into anything ethereal, exempt from any connection with the organic or any dependence on it. Certainly it is transcendental in regard to organic action since it can direct it, but first of all it is subject to it. It is autonomous, but its autonomy is neither unconditioned nor boundless.

For it is conditioned by the non-voluntary dynamisms that it meets in a given personality, and it is bounded by the limitations of those dynamisms. No one is in a position to do anything whatever at any moment whatever. It is inaccurate to say a man does what he likes; rather, he does what he can. In a word, human freedom is not the equal of divine freedom. To express this we say it is "situated" and "engaged", and we speak of its being "caught in the toils" of matter and situation.

(3) We stressed the receptive side of voluntary action. But that is not the whole question. For voluntary action in utilizing the non-voluntary also acts upon it and transforms its potential.

A suggestive analogy is that of grafting. The simile is valid at several points. First of all it illustrates the duality which must not be lost sight of. We have to distinguish between the shoot and the stock on to which it is grafted. They are things of different kinds. We may observe—though this is a secondary factor—that compared to the stock, the shoot is at first, in most cases, something minute, almost a negligible quantity. We need hardly go into more explicit detail to show the appropriateness of the analogy.

But what is the reason for grafting? It is done in order that the already living shoot may borrow its vital principle from the stock, that is, from something different from itself. A communication of vital elements is set up, and the grafted shoot is the first to benefit. Henceforth the life of the stock constitutes the environment in which it will live and grow. Moreover the vicissitudes which may come upon the stock will have their repercussions on the life of the shoot. Here we have something comparable to the incarnation of voluntary action.

But a fresh element appears, and a most important one: the

grafted shoot does not merely borrow the stock's vital forces and stop at that; it transforms and transposes them. It uses *in its own way* forces which initially were not its own, and makes the stock bear fruit which alone it would never have produced. It draws out of it more than was ever in it; it enlarges its potential. And by that means the intended vital integration becomes complete.

That is how we need to understand the utilization of the non-voluntary by volition. Not as a tool, remaining something apart from the agent using it: for integration occurs. We are already acquainted with the passive, receptive aspect of the voluntary: it borrows. But to borrow is already an act. And it borrows *in its own way*: it transforms what it borrows. Its receptivity is not to be denied (in the old days there was a tendency to deny it, no doubt in order to safeguard all the merits of the free act), but it is active receptivity. Let us be more precise and say it is conscious and selective receptivity.

Conscious receptivity, because it is aware of what it is borrowing, aware of the energies it is drawing upon, and the mechanisms it is employing. And this awareness is indispensable in order that the receptivity may be selective, that is to say, capable of *yes* and *no*. In human acts choice is not really creative; that is only strictly true of divine freedom. Choice is above all conscious acceptance. Thus we come to a very important point: it is the essence of the free act that we discover; and now it must be placed in its context, that of personal consent, deliberate welcome, positive or negative acquiescence. That is what freedom in the psychological sense consists in.

It is fundamental to describe the human free act in this way, because its double aspect, passive and active, is maintained and underlined. We can only accept what already exists independently of the act of acceptance, at least at the moment when the question arises (for I can accept myself); but in relation to something other than myself, one of two attitudes is possible: acceptance or rejection; yes, or no. That is the form in which we first meet freedom. So to be psychologically free is to be capable of this conscious acceptance, this personal consent, this conscious and deliberate adhesion. What do we consent to? Precisely this: a non-voluntary factor whether within us or outside.

(4) The essence of the free act lies, as we said, in personal consent. But let us not go on to deduce that that alone is free. Our analogy is still relevant: the graft utilizes the sap of the stock in its own way, it turns it into a sap of the species to which it belongs. In the same way, anything involuntary in me becomes free the moment I consent to it; it is assumed by my ego and transposed on to its plane. No matter what its origin, whatever is selectively and consciously accepted becomes free. Take, for instance, mother-love. We know how its roots go down into the instinctive depths: it is founded principally on hormones. So that in theory it might happen that the care with which a given woman surrounded her child remained on the plane of instinctive impulses. Does that mean that mother-love is simply and always instinctive?—It must not be forgotten that a woman becomes conscious of the impulses of this instinct of hers; so she can consent to them in full awareness. Their source remains instinctive; but what of that? Her personal acquiescence places her actions on another plane. A mother acts freely, she consciously lets instinct run its course inside her, she admits its proposals and acts in accordance with them in full awareness of what she is doing and by this means all her maternal activity (the totality of the acts thus prompted) becomes free.

Thus it is inopportune to submit freedom of action to too precise an analysis which would end in cutting it down to practically nothing. For an example of an analysis of this kind, take the steam train, which, as is evident, produces its own energy in order to move. One might start looking for what it is in the train that really *moves*. The railway carriages would be eliminated one by one, till finally only the engine remained: the engine is what really moves. To submit the free act to this treatment would lead to the elimination of everything that happened spontaneously, necessarily. And in the last resort there would not remain much of a free act: it would be that infinitely brief, almost imperceptible moment of consent, of adhesion. To proceed thus is to identify live things with fabricated ones, and to explain what is living by what has no life of its own. It is to fall into an error which has been pointed out so often: for in non-living things heteroclite elements are juxtaposed; whereas where there is life, on the contrary an integration takes place which brings the assimilated element on to a different plane, making it belong to a different order of things; thus non-living food becomes living flesh; in nutritional processes what is purely physical is raised to the physiological plane.

In the free act, the acceptance, slight as it may be in itself, makes the whole spontaneous action free, truly free. There occurs a veritable assumption of spontaneous, non-voluntary mechanisms. So that one might say, without paradox, that what is necessary becomes free, and that there is a transmutation from determinism into freedom.

What a long way we have come from our initial contrasts, so neat and clear, purely conceptual as they were—necessity versus freedom, passivity versus activity, dependence versus autonomy. Once grafted on to the non-voluntary, volition draws from it both its vitality and its efficacity, and it even turns non-volition into volition. So we see how extremely wary we have to be in attempting to comprehend freedom of action if we want to avoid coming to grief.

II. FREEDOM—AND LIBERTIES

The presence of necessity at the very heart of the free act engenders other confusions.

The words "freedom" and "liberty" have acquired extensions of meaning in common parlance, the latter seeming to crop up more frequently in the plural form than in the singular. This plural is sufficient witness to the fact that the word is being used derivatively. It is fairly frequently observed that derivative meanings, being more easily grasped, and more obvious, encroach on the original meaning, obscuring it and relegating it to second place. So much so that for many people the affirmation or denial, in any given case, of a particular liberty, is automatically equivalent to the assertion or negation of liberty, or freedom, as such, that is, freedom in the psychological sense.

What gives rise to these derivative meanings are the multiple determinants which are liable to be imposed on human activity. In the long run, there are as many liberties as there are forms of determinism, whether of a physical or physiological order, or psychic, or social.

One or other of these liberties is said to exist when the determinisms indispensable to the positing of a given action lie at our disposal. The absence of the latter would imply the negation of the corresponding liberty. We will look at negative cases first because they seem to be the most frequent, for when people talk of liberties it is usually to point out their non-existence. Afterwards we will take cases where the presence of *one* liberty permits us to infer the presence of *freedom*.

First, we may state that a paralysed man is not free to walk: his nerves and muscles, agents of his walking, are deficient. A prisoner is not free to leave his cell: his physical strength, even supported by all the ingenuity he can muster, is not able to break down the resistance of the walls, doors and windows of his gaol. A neurasthenic patient is not free to believe himself sinful: psychic mechanisms incite in him an obsessive conviction of culpability. A subordinate is not, as such, free to expatiate to his superior on his grievances or desires: at least such outspoken behaviour would constitute a grave risk for the man who indulged in it. Social custom, whether defensible or not, would not tolerate it. All these cases can be expressed uniformly by saying, "He is not free to . . .".

Is all freedom excluded? Not at all. We are dealing with liberties, not psychic freedom. Given conditions render such and such behaviour, or such and such a state, either impossible or necessary. But they do not touch basic freedom at all; not the one that man, as conscious being, possesses in himself, not the one that permits him to take up a personal attitude to this inevitable situation. A prisoner might be freely a captive: he has but to accept his condition and acquiesce in it. A paralytic, a neurasthenic, while undergoing treatment and hoping for renewed health, may consent to his infirmity: then he posits a free act, which does not however reduce the ineluctable character of his state. Again, fully aware of the risks he runs, a subordinate may freely decide to speak out or hold his tongue.

So when we observe the absence of a particular liberty in any given case, we have no right whatever to declare that psychic freedom is therefore absent too. This very important distinction is often overlooked. Yet in the field of moral temptation it is what enables a man to tell the difference between temptation and fault. Sometimes, through disregarding the distinction, people accuse themselves of a non-existent sin, whereas other people, in order to avoid confessing a real one, refuse to admit the distinction, or pretend to be unaware of it.

There are different liberties, different forms of freedom, corresponding to the different determinisms inherent in freedom of action. Let us add to the series a special one with no determinism attached to it: moral freedom. Obviously it is closely connected with moral obligation, but the latter is no necessity. That is why we deliberately left it out when we were enumerating the forms of determinism with which freedom has to come to terms.

This brings us to a point well worth considering: absence of moral freedom tends to become identified with absence of psychic freedom. There are many legions of men and women who, because they know they are obliged to perform a certain action, conclude that it can no longer be freely done. To the question: "Are we free to attend Mass on Sundays?" the usual answer will be, "We are not free because the Church makes an obligation of it"; with scant deference to logic, this quickly becomes, "We don't go to church on Sundays of our own accord". Be it said in passing, that is no doubt why so many Christians are so little concerned to make it a truly free act. There is confusion, of course: the obligation eliminates a liberty, it removes the moral freedom to do or not do something. But the actual freedom to perform the act has not vanished at all. In fact the obligation itself only exists because I am psychologically free, and in so far as I am free. To obey an order is a free act so long as it is not solely the fruit of necessity, moral necessity as it is called. But many people see it differently and conclude that only by refusing to obey an order are they acting freely.

So we see how the derivative meanings attached to the notion of freedom give rise to equivocation: more precisely, they provoke a denial of psychic freedom when a particular liberty is absent. *Liberties* confuse people's idea of *freedom*.

The converse is also true. It may come about that we affirm the free character of an act erroneously: illusions about freedom do exist, and it is a problem that psychologists are

4

specially interested in at the moment: depth psychology has done a great deal to bring it into the light of day.

People are certainly capable of believing they are acting freely when their action is simply the result of an irresistible complex. Such cases may even be numerous. The victims are the scrupulous and the neurotic.

An illusion of this sort may also derive from a "disin-carnate" conception of freedom. Those who are unaware of the bondage of the human will do not understand the bounds that limit its activity either. For example, some people when they are unable to do what they had proposed accuse them-selves of laziness. Others will claim to have given a matter due and free consideration, when all they did was to accept it on sight. They will affirm that they came to certain ideas voluntarily, whereas it was association or some psychic pro-cess that engendered them in their minds. They will believe their feelings are voluntary ones, when they are due to circumstance alone. These are all cases of over-rapid identifi-cation of consciousness with freedom. To become aware of something going on inside us is not yet to admit it or consent to it. It is not assumed at the freedom level. It remains unfree.

Finally, there is a rather unexpected juncture to note. If necessity and freedom can combine in a single human action, an illusion about freedom, and authentic freedom, may also criss-cross within one and the same piece of behaviour. If we track down an illusion as to the freedom of a given act, we may still not take it as proven that there is no authentic free-dom there. In a recent article Father Rimaud puts a question and leaves it unanswered: "Modern propaganda technique being what it is, where is freedom of thought?"—We will accept the challenge and demonstrate that it would be wrong to believe that propaganda destroys freedom of thought. No doubt it puts it to the test pretty severely; we will come to that later. It shifts the point of application, but it is not the death-knell of freedom of thought.

What the author evidently had in mind is a fact well known to collective psychology; opinion can be prefabricated. The influence of social environment is so strong, it works so intensively and with such a sure touch, that many of the opinions we put forward are merely the result of suggestion. We find them inside us, we become aware of them, and we conclude that we produced them ourselves.

Let us be very practical. Take the housewife, for instance, who holds that X's soap is better than Y's. Or the smoker persuaded that so-and-so's cigarettes are the finest. There we have opinions. Those who express them are convinced that they think as they do of their own free will. Father Rimaud, on the other hand, wonders whether freedom of thought is present at all. His query is certainly not without cogency.

Indeed, a full answer cannot be given without making a distinction. Let us distinguish, on the one hand, the opinion which the housewife holds, and on the other, its source of origin. Taking the second point first, we find that freedom of thought is most probably an illusion. The housewife will doubtless insist that it was entirely her own idea: she is convinced of the superiority of her kind of soap because she tried it out and experience produced convincing facts: whiter sheets, less work, quicker results, and so on—all the outcome of practical observation, justifying a free and personal opinion.

Now we come to the other side of the picture. Is the critical psychologist dismayed by the insistent tone of the advertisement? Far from it: it is to him one more proof that social suggestion does its job. The advertiser's multifarious and ingenious reiterations have, he declares, predisposed the housewife to discover, or recognize, in his wares the vaunted excellence. The influence of publicity is preponderant. In actual fact, though unwittingly, the housewife was biased in favour of the product: thus the illusion of verification comes into being. For, says the psychologist, you will admit that there is no way of totting up and measuring all the features concerned, so any judgments formed can only be arbitrary ones. That makes it all the easier for suggestion to do its work. Subjectively, there is quite a sincere conviction of superior quality, no one would want to deny that. It is the underlying objective elements which are so dubious. We ourselves side with the psychologist, granting that non-voluntary mechanisms—belonging here to the psychic order—worked together to furnish the true motivation. As far as the source of her opinions is concerned, the housewife's freedom of thought is illusory.

But does it follow that freedom is completely absent, and that nothing in her opinion is free? That is not self-evident. Let us bring housewife and psychologist face to face with one another, and let us suppose that the housewife sticks to her opinion. She may be somewhat shaken, at least inwardly, by the psychologist's careful elucidations. Running over in her mind the circumstances in which she thought she had observed the vaunted results, she will admit that her methods of reaching a conclusion were somewhat hazy, and that she might perhaps have been more consistent. But she does not change her mind. She still sticks to her opinion and continues thinking as she did before. And that is how an opinion can be freely accepted and freely stated, even if its original source was suggestion, and even if this fact is admitted. The idea was not formed freely, the person concerned is aware of it, but none the less gives his assent to it freely; or at least he freely adheres to it. So the technique of propaganda does not abolish all freedom of thought. It enlarges the range and scope of suggestion, and it often reduces freedom to a simple acceptance of current opinion.

The reader may consider I have cut my argument a little short. Could one not, in fact, attribute the upholding of an opinion to another determinant: pig-headedness for instance? Clearly, one can imagine a whole train of successive determinants. But that is not where the root of the question lies. As soon as a person has become aware of the existence and influence of one or more non-voluntary mechanisms, he is in a position to posit a free act of acceptance or rejection. And this constitutes a free decision about non-voluntary factors. Of course the number of determinants involved does not matter at all. However commonplace, the example chosen is none the less typical. Social environment furnished the unconscious motivation of ideas, then actions. But unconscious motivation may spring from other sources. One's individual psychical make-up may be one, or the unconscious itself, for instance: it can produce opinions which you will first take for freely-formed ones, so much so that you will need dissuading and persuading of the contrary. But afterwards you may still freely adhere to the same opinions. And things can get even more complicated: you may think you deliberately hold an opinion when it is merely present in your mind. Everyone knows how a stomach-ache can focus attention on itself, but few realize how an idea can impose itself on the mind, or it may be an impression or an emotion. If necessary, this has to be pointed out, and as a general rule it is as well to forgo the conclusion that we are always free the moment we are clearly conscious. But that is no reason for falling into the opposite extreme and deciding that we are never free.

If we were now to round off our dissertation by hymning the rights and wrongs of this state of things, we should stray from our course. Indeed, all we wanted to do was to point out that freedom does not necessarily disappear for good, though we admit that for many people freedom is confined to "letting things happen".

III. HUMAN FREEDOM—INELUCTABLE FREEDOM

You may object that "letting things happen" is no longer a free act, for the dynamic element, the one that starts an action off, is surely independent of personality, even if it is inherent. In reality this decisive factor is always present. No external cause, whether of a social or of a psychical order, can incite an act except through the intermediary of the physiological or psychical mechanisms which it may stimulate. In such cases, indeed, a man does not act, he is acted upon. You may insist that in order to "let things happen" no clear consciousness is necessary.

This we must concede: "letting things happen" demands no personal effort, and no reflection either. The possibility of full freedom is excluded. But if we come back to the question: Does this imply a total absence of freedom?—the answer is, No. We may not lose sight of the fact that man can make a twofold use of his freedom.

Let us adopt the expressions "stronger form", and "weaker form" of freedom, to clarify this point.

When we discuss freedom, it is generally the former that we have in mind. It implies lucidity of the critical faculty and control over the impulses urging action. The person in question not only knows where he is going, he is clearly aware of it, and thus the way is open for a consent positively given, in full knowledge of the facts. Obviously, an empirical proof of the existence of freedom could only be obtained on the assumption of its stronger form.

But if we consider the *incarnation* of the human will, we can understand that other use of freedom which, for lack of a better name, we call its weaker form. There is a whole infra-conscious, non-voluntary dynamism of multiple aspects seething within us, without our connivance. But, being free, the will is at least to a certain extent capable of utilizing these dynamisms, accepting or rejecting them in part or in whole. And this utilization will depend on the values which the will intends to pursue. One among those values is worth mentioning because it is peculiarly adapted to engendering the second form of free activity: this is easy-goingness, to which Ricœur has devoted a penetrating scrutiny. It solicits the will and presents itself as a value well worth pursuing. With the result that it is attracted to what is easily done; it permits obstacles to be circumvented or partially reduced. For instance, the customary is attractive for the reason that, once established, it furnishes the line of least resistance. To avoid confusion, let us say that although easy-goingness may include a germ of laziness, it does not necessarily predispose to inactivity. The reason for this is plain, for our dynamisms urge us to action spontaneously, of their own accord, following their own bent. Not to act, or to react but slightly, is far from being the easier course. Inactivity might be due to easy-goingness, but only eventually, when with advancing years the spontaneous urges grow less keen. It is easy for a man of seventy to rest in his armchair; for a child of four or five it is very difficult to sit still and what comes easily to him is running about and dashing up and down stairs. Thus easy-goingness promotes moderate exercise of the various dynamisms. The implicit motto would seem to be, not "do nothing" but "let things happen", whether through the agency of the immediate environment, following fashion and current opinion, or through that of submerged impulses. The potential field of extension is very great, it can spread to give play to nearly all our tendencies; and it can create its own characteristic attitude to life in general.

The pursuit of ease thus has claims of its own on human activity. Clearly it will not of its own accord incite to the use of freedom in its stronger form. No great concentration or effort is needed just to let things go their course, even when one is personally concerned. For instance, more effort is required on the part of a motorist to drive his car properly than merely to put his foot down and let it rip. To get a man moving one need not even move a foot: the spontaneous tendencies take care of that, stimulating action by sheer dint of functioning naturally. For all that, we may not believe that freedom has entirely ceased to intervene. The pursuit of ease keeps a lot of different urges on tap, as we saw. So choice and adherence still have a part to play. In man, values never occur one at a time; at every moment of the day several tendencies solicit his attention. Taking the easier course will involve satisfying now one, now another; taking now this direction, now that, as absence of impediment suggests. The diversity of the impulses remains. Choosing the easier course means rejecting the rest, even if it is only because doing that is easier than coping with the other urges. By putting it back into its proper context we discover that easy-goingness, though allowing for conscious appraisal, has a reverse side: a withdrawal from other possible acts, in particular those which would demand a more virile use of the will.

The easy-going ways of a free person may not be likened to an animal's unconstraint, where its very nature is to yield to preponderating urges. The whole context is a different one. In both, attraction is non-voluntary in origin, but in man a reluctance to give his will full play must also be taken into account. And it is this attitude towards free activity in the stronger sense, that seems essentially to constitute the weaker form of freedom. Thus deviously easy-goingness still comes under the jurisdiction of freedom. Tied down to nature as it is, freedom is ineluctable in a being capable of conscious activity. It is in a way atmospheric: it embraces all human activity. Even when hidden, it is still present. Man cannot evade it.

In problems concerning the moral life it is often necessary

to take this weaker form of freedom into consideration. It comes to light in an analysis of the sinner's psychology. Most of the sins people admit to are, after all, sins of omission. Which means that in general behaviour the really sinful moment is the moment of omission. We are not claiming that it is so for all sins: some do really belong to the stronger form of free activity; but it is evidently not the case for every kind of sin. As someone said, "No man is intentionally wicked". Very few want to sin, but many resign themselves to it because it is the easy-going way out of their difficulties. In describing the sinful soul St Bernard remarked, "It is a soul both bound and free; bound because of the necessity (to which it yields), free because of the will. And what is still more striking, and still more disastrous, it is culpable by reason of being free, and thus, bound by reason of being free."[1] Sin implies an attraction due to the spontaneous play of urges but soliciting the will. A fault has its original source in the non-voluntary. But the will, though it could, made no effort, it gave in. The total, plenary adhesion which would constitute the stronger form of voluntary activity was lacking. Total adhesion is possible, but it is pretty rare. More often the yielding is done by omission, because it is easier. Assent is conceded out of laxity or indulgence. But to resign and withdraw is still the act of a free being. When a mayor resigns from office, he loses all the privileges attached to it. When we resign our freedom we do not as a consequence lose our freedom, we remain free. For our resignation still took place within our freedom. There is never complete estrangement: and that is how the weaker form of freedom is accounted for.

Freedom remains at the source of more than one of the passions tainted with moral culpability. To each and every passion there is an abnormal stress, a proliferation of the demands of an urge. It is not difficult to perceive how deliberate

[1] St Bernard, *Serm. in Cant.*, 81, No. 9.

non-interference, free-and-easy ways, lack of constraint, produce conditions favourable to the burgeoning and blossoming of a passion. Who is tomorrow's drunkard? The man who has a dry throat today. When your throat is dry, the simplest thing to do is to quench your thirst. Among possible thirst-quenchers, one, alcoholic drink, is found to be the most agreeable and perhaps the most effective. The easiest course is to absorb a lot of it. Repeated practice engenders habit by specifying need, and the drunkard is the man who, when thirsty, desires to quench his thirst with alcohol and nothing else. Yielding to the easy course turned him into an addict. The origin of all evil must be sought in non-voluntary dynamisms when voluntary activity in its stronger form is not mustered to deal with them.

Ultimately one may say that the moral life and the religious life encounter no peril greater than this risk to which a demise of the will exposes them.

Freedom is not an end in itself. It is a means which a human being has at his disposal to help forge his personality as a man and a Christian. This progressive personalization runs exactly parallel to the growth in freedom in which liberation consists. We forget this all too often. Freedom grows; it is no complete and perfect gift from the beginning. Initial freedom is but a seedling: its destiny is to grow and expand. Its progress will lead to a more or less complete control of the determinisms, till at last these become the supple instruments of an ordered will.

Man has to win this control by conquest. The non-voluntary is paramount in his ordinary behaviour. The will has its roots there and only gradually emerges, its power is at first pretty insignificant, for the will is still captive. It is up to it to extend its hold, loosen its bonds, liberate itself; not by shaking off the non-voluntary, or annihilating it—indeed, the will cannot become "disincarnate" without being the victim of its own victory—but by humanizing it more, making it better and better able to serve the expansion of the Christian life. Such liberation is not the liberation of the will alone but of the whole human automatism, which reaches its fulfilment under the ægis of the will. The initial duality is not suppressed, but it is surmounted through the integration of the "necessary" in a life now properly human and Christian.

Nothing can be done to bring about this emancipation save a lucid, courageous and persevering exercise of the will. Easygoingness marks an inverse movement, it operates the other way round. It allows the non-voluntary to gain ground and gather strength: so a man will be at the beck and call of deterministic impulses which overstress the bogged-down state of volition and block the action of liberation and consequent personalization. In moral progress, nothing more can be expected of a will that is running down, or a freedom that has no intention of taking on its responsibilities.

As for the Christian, he awaits his deliverance by God and God will grant it. *Christus nos liberavit.* But as a Christian he has to collaborate with grace, accepting it implicitly and giving his personal consent to the inspiration of the Spirit. Even redeemed and restored by Christ, the free will always remains at grips with the allurements of the "flesh", "nature", which in St Paul's broad interpretation is equivalent to the "non-voluntary" in us. *"Ne libertatem in occasionem detis carnis."*[1] But the supreme liberation to which the Spirit would bring it does not, for the Christian, consist in the selfish exaltation of his individual potentialities, it is, once more, submission and service, the service of God and fellow men, but now in charity; this means conscious, joyful giving, and an alienation of selfhood that is perfectly free and totally liberating; the great apostle St Paul shows us how it is done: *"Cum liber essem ex omnibus, omnium me servum feci, ut plures lucrifacerem."*[2]

[1] Gal. v. 13.   [2] I Cor. ix. 19.

III

THE SENSE OF SIN AND ITS DEVIATIONS

By Canon Jean Vieujean
Professor at the University of Louvain

I. THE MODERN WORLD AND THE SENSE OF SIN

SOME little time ago, a cartoon appeared in a Belgian daily newspaper: it pictured a classroom with a very worried-looking teacher standing on the right; on the left a boy was prostrate on the floor, and in the middle another child, murder in his eyes, was still brandishing the tell-tale mallet with which he had felled his victim. Near him, half-kneeling, with a protective hand on the culprit's shoulder, a psychiatric assistant turned to the teacher saying, "The main thing is, not to give him a guilt complex, isn't it !"

Here we have a humorous caricature of a whole current of ideas that percolates devastatingly through the modern world: ready to cry down and perhaps abolish the sense of sin and consequently the sense of responsibility.

This is an extremely serious state of affairs. For in the problem of responsibility and sin the whole human person is engaged. Man knows himself as man by the fact that he is a free and responsible conscious being, capable of being left on his own and accountable for himself. Man is a moral being, whose only worth lies in his moral growth, and not at all in the abundance of his knowledge or the power of his technical achievements. In the problem of responsibility is implicated the very essence of religion, particularly the Christian religion, teaching as it does that man's destiny is fulfilled by living participation in a supreme Being—God—from whom sin separates us, and that man only regains access to God by disavowing his fault, renouncing sin, humbly and lovingly adhering to a Saviour, Jesus Christ.

Intrinsically, and on account of his human condition, there is a more or less lively feeling of responsibility and guilt in every man. And that is, basically, the hardest thing he has to bear. It is his foremost problem, in which he is aware that everything is at stake; the one that explains his metaphysical or existential anguish and the sense of solitude which, to a greater or lesser degree, is the lot of every human being.

No wonder man tries to escape and seeks to be delivered from this condition. Two main ways lie open to him, the first is to deny that sin and responsibility exist and attempt to discard the feeling of guilt by declaring it fundamentally morbid. Let us state at once that we consider this way utterly fatal to the exalted dignity of the human person. The second way is to accept the human condition, purifying and cleansing one's sense of responsibility as part of the process of cultivating it, and considering the moral effort to be the very essence of a man's life. "Ill or well, a human being knows only one fundamental problem: the problem of good and evil", as De Greeff put it. For man is called to achieve integration by sheer dint of wrestling with his inner tensions and stresses. *Militia est vita hominis super terram.*[1]

In the world today, a diminution of the sense of sin, even among Christians, is a phenomenon that moralists constantly remark upon. In former times, they declare, in the Middle Ages for instance, perhaps men sinned as much as they do today, but they did call their conduct sin. But now, for a century, sin has been out of date. "It is I who suppressed sin", said Renan.

Sin cannot be got rid of otherwise than by getting rid of

[1] Job vii. 1.

freedom and demonstrating that man, who has the illusion of being free, is in reality determined in all he does by forces of which he is unconscious.

In pagan antiquity, recourse was had chiefly to extrinsic causes. Sin was a sort of madness—a *paranoia*—sent to man by jealous gods or by fate, *moira*.

"When a mortal is working his own destruction, the gods come to his assistance", said Æschylus. But modern science has recourse to intrinsic causes in support of moral determinism.

Fifty years ago, science would chiefly invoke physical, organic, and biological forces. Good and evil were natural secretions, man was the plaything of his bio-chemical reactions, and we were no more responsible for our virtues and vices than beetroot for its sugar or belladona for its poison.

But in the last fifty years it is the discoveries concerning the human psyche which have impressed our contemporaries most. Let us mention three main ones.

The first is the influence of *hormones* on the psycho-moral behaviour of individuals. Hormones are substances secreted by glands and they stimulate biological functions which in their turn have a repercussion on psychic behaviour. The ancients would have called them "humours", with an influence on the "humour" or temperament of a person. "For instance, a little more or less thyroid hormone, either renal or sexual, produces an immediate alteration (that is to say, without delay or intermediary) in a man's zest for his work, courage under ordeal, or respect for another person's integrity", according to Biot. Anger, sloth, lust, greed, even pride, can now be said to depend on the state of my hormones, or so it is claimed. So how can I be blamed for yielding to those impulses? What virtue is there in resisting them? Vice and virtue are a function of my glands, and that is all there is to them. They are things to be dealt with if I am an amorphous element or a dangerous element in this world and need to be turned into a normally adapted member of society.

The second discovery was made in the course of certain neuro-surgical therapies which also exercise a profound influence on the human psyche. For instance someone has an incredible capacity for hard work, but is unfortunately always in such a state of excitement and agitation that it makes life quite unbearable for other people. An operation, prefrontal leucotomy (a severing of some of the white fibres connecting the anterior frontal cortex with the rest of the brain) is performed and lo and behold, if it is successful—after a period of psychic collapse—a new equilibrium is found, characterized by a great diminution of the former vital dynamism, but at least enabling the patient to live at peace with other people. There we have virtue regained at a stroke of the surgeon's lancet.

Thirdly, we have the discoveries of *psycho-analysis*, which reveal the important part the unconscious plays in our behaviour.

Take a homosexual who is arrested for misconduct with young boys. In the course of psycho-analysis it turns out that during his early childhood his mother inspired him with a horror of sexual life and put him on his guard to an excessive degree. Once married, he experienced a sense of shame in sexual relations with his wife, and his submerged instinct sought satisfaction in homosexuality. How far is he responsible?

Again, a boy was sent to boarding-school. He made no open protest but was none the less very unhappy at being separated from his parents, and in due course he shammed illness, though his health was excellent. Was this a deliberate intentional lie? Not at all: the boy subconsciously took refuge in illness.

Then there is the social climber. By pulling strings he got

himself appointed to a position manifestly beyond his powers. He behaved abominably to his subordinates. The reason being, not wicked perversity, but an inferiority complex and a repressed bad conscience lurking at the bottom of his unconscious and causing all the havoc.

The conclusion one is tempted to draw is, that our whole moral life is obscurely governed by the unconscious. Specifically, what we call unruly conduct, fault, sin, has its source, though we are unaware of it, in deep, uncontrollable regions of our being.

Psycho-analysis went even further, at least in the mind of its founder, Freud, and several of its protagonists. It claimed to strike at the root of the guilt-feeling by explaining the genesis of moral convictions, not by an intellectual intuition of right order and man's place in it, but by parental training and fear of society, and nothing else. For Freud, the sense of guilt comes from the Œdipus complex and constitutes a reaction from criminal desires to murder one's father and have sexual relations with one's mother. As he wrote, "We must remember that parricide and incest are the two greatest crimes that man can commit . . . and we must also remember that other investigations led us to the hypothesis that the conscience of mankind, which now appears as a power inherited in the mind, was originally acquired by the Œdipus complex".

As we see, the affirmation is categorical. For Freud and his orthodox disciples, morality (like religion, and art and science) is a product of the Super-Ego, that is to say, of an ideal self who comes into being through pressure of the Libido repressed by family or social taboos. Morality has no absolute or metaphysical value. It is not answerable to any transcendence.

All psycho-analyists are not as radical as that. Several, while accepting Freud's psycho-genetic explanations of morality, refuse to pronounce on its metaphysical and metapsychical origins. But we see why Freud's theories received a warm welcome from an enormous section of the public. They reduce morality to a positive arbitrary law. They turn the sense of guilt into the simple residue of an ancestral complex.

Finally, psycho-analysis has discredited the sense of guilt and made it suspect by revealing the part it plays in neuroses, seeing in it, if not the main source, at least an element accompanying all neuroses. As Hesnard wrote, "The symptoms of neurosis and psychosis *have a meaning*, a personal human significance, such that in his morbid behaviour the patient struggles against a formidable and ceaseless *indictment* and puts up a defence by all sorts of means. He lives in a virtual or real world of guilt. His whole existence unfolds under the sign of culpability".

The conclusions drawn differ in various authors.

The wise say: Let us distinguish between health and disease. There is a healthy sense of guilt, and let us cultivate it. There is a morbid one. Let us cure it.

A sense of guilt is a danger to man, say others, and still more so a sense of *sin*, which implies opposition to God, disobedience to an omnipotent Will, a breach with Absolute Good personified, and thus produces the distressing feeling of an existential catastrophe, a destiny gone wrong in its totality. All this adds to a fault committed an affective burden so dangerous to the psyche that it would be far better to suppress the idea of *sin* and simply keep that of a *fault*, considering it merely as an error of conduct harmful to the expansion of the self and destructive of social harmony. Thus we should retain the notion of the necessity of moral progress, but exorcise from our faults the metaphysical anguish that accompanies them when we see them as sin. Morality without sin!

Yet others want to go further still, like Freud and his more loyal supporters. Morality is a simple superstructure created by the Super-Ego. Its prescriptions are purely arbitrary and valueless, though some of them are useful for family and social reasons. They come into the category of taboos.

All these ideas are current. The scientific truths they contain, and the abuses in interpretation to which they are liable, are immediately apparent. Thrown to the public at large, picked up without reflection or discrimination, they constitute one of the greatest perils in existence for men of our time. In reality, man experiences a great need for justification. And now at last he can be just in his own eyes without having to take too much trouble over it, and be delivered at a good bargain price from the burden of his personal responsibility and remorse. The glands did it. Hormones upset his equilibrium. It is all due to a morbid guilt complex. Good-bye, sense of sin. And good-bye, moral effort—for most people.

II. THE CHRISTIAN SENSE OF SIN

What Christianity thinks of sin shall now be recapitulated in nine propositions.

(1) Christianity believes in man's *liberty* and responsibility. In the human person it sees an incomplete being, answerable for himself, and expected to proceed towards his own perfection. It believes in the possibility for man consciously and voluntarily to stray from his "vocation", and thus to fail. It believes in original sin as the initial cause and the principal cause of the ills that afflict the world.

(2) Christianity sees in man a being involved in *relations*, natural ones appropriate to his status as creature, and supernatural ones, as son by adoption, *with God*. These relations are made known to him through reason on the one hand, faith on the other. Christianity sees in man's life an event that is enacted principally and mysteriously between man and God.

If man subordinates his life to God, he will find God and in Him he will find his own perfect fulfilment. If he turns away from God and persists in his aversion, he is radically lost, he fails in his destiny. For Christianity, a breach in morality is not only a blunder, an error, a folly, an infringement of the world's harmony, not only social disorder, or lack of humanism: it is something that happens between man and God. It is, indeed, what we call *sin*.

By revealing the existence between God and ourselves of relations of an inconceivable intimacy, by increasing within us the sense of God's presence and the sense of our freedom, Christianity has intensified the sense of sin. It has turned sin into an act affecting our relations with God, breaking into the intimacy of persons united by close bonds; an act against Love; and thus it has given sin its true dimension: superhuman, infinite. Sin is an insult to God, an attack on Love.

(3) Christianity believes in the gravity of sin precisely because it has an exalted conception of the human person, which it holds to be conscious, free, autonomous, responsible, supernaturalized, saved and dwelt in by God Himself, called to live eternally with Him and in Him. To diminish the metaphysical gravity of sin is to strike at the human person itself.

To deal with sin is to deal with the quintessence of Christianity. For sin is at the heart of the drama between man and God that has been unfolding since the beginning of the world. Sin is at the heart of Christ's mission and Redemption. It is at the heart of the Church's mission and the Sacraments. The essence of Christianity is grace, is love, is the expansion of the whole man in a more and more lively participation in the world, in other men, in God. But sin is precisely the loss of grace, the ruin of love, the destruction of living contacts. Henceforth sin is the main foe to be combated, it is man's supreme evil.

(4) Far from seeking to attenuate the sense of responsibility, or wrongdoing, or sin, Christianity tries to intensify it. Awareness of sin occupies a vital place in the person of Jesus. He himself was totally exempt from moral evil. But sin constantly occupied his mind. It was for sinners that he came, it was to save what was lost, it was to take on himself the sins of the world, and finally to expiate them on the cross.

This lively consciousness of sin Jesus hoped to see in His disciples too. To a sinner Jesus never said, "It is nothing". He was friendly and forgiving, but His call to order was imperious: "Go and sin no more." He exhorts us all to watch and pray, not to enter into temptation, to be delivered from evil. He urges us with the utmost vigour to flee all occasion of sin, to tear from us whatever may be the source of sins, even things essential to our natural life. He requires us to do penance, or we shall risk eternal perdition. Not for a moment does He conceal from us that our fate is in our own hands.

This lively awareness of sin is found again in the best of the Christians, that is, the saints. One of the universal signs of holiness is a sense of the horror of sin and the need to expiate and make reparation. Whereas the more remote holiness is, the more the sense of sin is attenuated and fades away and vanishes.

(5) While affirming the existence of free will, Christian moralists know well that man's freedom is not absolute but relative, that it is at grips with physiological and psychical determinisms, both conscious and unconscious, and with external pressure from family and society. It is a limited, relative freedom, an initial embryonic freedom, with a mission gradually to create itself, for the sake of the Good and with the help of the Good. Freedom, wounded by original sin and personal sins, is faced with the task of undertaking to

cure itself, utilizing the means that nature and grace put at its disposal.

Obviously it is only wholly responsible for what it chooses in the full light of day and brings about fully consenting. On that account subjective guilt is often less than the actual fault. Now this is an important and delicate factor to take into account in appreciating people's conduct and furthering their moral education. But there is nothing here to imply the non-existence of sin, or exempt anyone from the obligation of seeking light and strength for the inevitable struggle.

(6) The *discoveries* of modern science in physiology and psychology have revealed the influence of certain bio-chemical elements (hormones) or psychic elements (the unconscious, the Super-Ego) on man's behaviour and on disorders of his psyche. Here moralists and spiritual directors manifest excessive distrust. In spite of the fanciful interpretations and the build-up of unacceptable theories that they have occasioned, these factors are well worth knowing and taking into account in estimating the moral worth of human behaviour; so that the collaboration of the doctor may be sought when needed. He may be able to remedy certain deficient psyches by a physical or psychical intervention (or a psychiatrical or psycho-analytical one). In numerous cases, the psyche needs curing of a false feeling of guilt in order to become accessible to an authentic sense of responsibility.

(7) The true moral worth of a man, the one he has in God's eyes, does not ultimately depend on the quality of his psyche. *It depends above all on what he achieves with the psyche he has.* "The searcher of hearts and reins is God." God alone knows what a man is worth, and what is his secret relation with Him. We do not know the degree of guilt that the weaknesses and faults of a deformed psyche (e.g. in a homosexual or an

alcoholic) represent in the eyes of God, nor what true moral value the "virtuous" actions of a healthy psyche represent. As for holiness, it is a secret between man and God, the mysterious act of a human soul opening out and offering itself to the transfiguring love of God. A healthy psyche can remain closed to God, complacent and self-satisfied in what it calls its honesty. A neurotic psyche can open out to God, all the more so for being aware of insufficiency and weakness.

This is not to say that we should neglect to heal sick psyches. Naturally, it is the psyche in a state as near perfection as possible that should be open to freedom and grace, and the burden men bear when afflicted with a deficient psyche, and the burden they so often constitute for those among whom they live, should be alleviated as far as possible.

(8) To stimulate man to a more and more perfect moral life, it is desirable that three things should grow to maturity in him:

(*a*) An increasing lucidity of conscience: not only better and better to discern the good to be done, but to get rid of inferior motives and motions that more or less consciously mingle with even the purest intentions. Purify the source: how the Gospel insists on it! We have to keep ourselves awake, watchful for God's hour, ready to seize every opportunity for good, behaving like trusty stewards, giving ourselves wholly to what we are doing, and avoiding the fecklessness of the girls in the parable. In short, by reflection and concentration, we have to shape our conscience inside us, and make it into a watchful, clarified, purified one. "It is not the will that has the primacy in man's life, it is knowledge, mind, conscience" (I. Klug).

(*b*) Great will power. To see the good is obviously not enough, it has to be done. Moreover, lucidity and faithfulness act and react the one upon the other. We have to do the truth if we want to attain to more light.

(c) A powerful, coherent system of values: ends to meditate upon and pursue; ideals to be realized—personal, family, social and religious ones; a more and more fervent and lively consecration of self to our fellows and to God. The twofold commandment of Love!

(9) Among these values is one which has constantly to be called to mind, and which constitutes the whole of Christianity: the redemptive Love of God and Jesus Christ. The sense of sin must never become parted from the sense of redemption. Christianity is salvation accomplished by the death and resurrection of the incarnate Word. To be a Christian is to believe that yielding to Christ and consenting to His healing—even when afflicted with the most deformed psyche, even after committing the most monstrous sins— means the renewal of our whole existence, right down to the spiritual roots of our being. Humble confession and absolution are all that are needed for salvation. Salvation—this is one of the most difficult conceptions to get people to admit, even Christians. And yet it is of primary importance in counterbalancing a man's awareness of sin and safeguarding him from the psychic disorders likely to arise from a sense of guilt which is separated from the awareness of redemption.

III. NORMAL GUILT AND MORBID GUILT

In spite of all this, the fact remains that the guilt feeling is one of the most liable to deviate into pathological states or neuroses or even psychoses.

Hesnard asserts, as we saw, that a feeling of guilt is present in one form or another in all neuroses. He considers it to be not the sole cause but an ever-present element. "Mental patients—from simple neuropaths to confirmed psychopaths —all give the impression of being victims of an accusation, that is, an allegation of sin directed at their person as being the one responsible." We must admit that we are *a priori* very distrustful of such generalizations. When a psychologist makes a "discovery", he instinctively tends to treat it as the long-lost secret of the universe and use it to explain the world. Like Freud with his Libido, who believed he held the clue not only to man but to the whole of history. They are, as someone said, "fantastic extrapolations", and we might add, "interpretive delirium".

Hesnard's work is remarkable on account of his clinical observations and many of his psychical analyses, but his conception of the world, and his interpretation of the facts, are governed by outright dialectical materialism, taken axiomatically.

Still, there is no doubt that many neuroses do have a sense of guilt at their origin, and all have one as a component, whether founded or not, or conscious or unconscious.

All this can be studied in detail in any standard textbook on psychiatry. We need only recall that neuroses are psychic disturbances due sometimes to somatic, sometimes to psychic causes (often both) of which the patient is aware. They differ in this respect from psychoses, which involve genuine mental alienation. Among the more common neuroses we may mention anxiety, inferiority feelings, hypochondria, phobias, obsessional neuroses, scruples, neurasthenia, hysteria.

It is not really surprising that the sense of guilt leads to deviations and is easily corrupted in a weak or traumatic psyche. The higher a value is, the more susceptible it is to corruption. Think of the distortions so often inflicted on values like love, freedom, or religion. In the moral life— which Christianity links so closely to freedom, love and religion—we have what we might call the supreme value. No wonder the guilt feeling sometimes becomes neurotic in a psyche predisposed to neurosis. Indeed we all have personal experience of how excessive fatigue or slight nervous depression exacerbate the sense of guilt and provoke hesitations, doubts, scruples and a feeling of inferiority towards the people to be encountered and the job to be done.

Further, even in a normal man, a constant effort is needed, on the one hand to avoid amorality and preserve a lucid and lively sense of sin, and on the other, to keep clear of a gloomy morbid feeling of culpability. There is nothing surprising about it. Sin is itself a disorder, it is irrational behaviour, it is folly. No wonder that it can have such harmful repercussions on the psyche, and that interior equilibrium is only regained by humbly repenting. To repeat De Greeff: "Ill or well, a human being knows only one fundamental problem, the problem of good and evil."

Between the healthy, normal, rational Christian sense of sin and the wholly morbid feeling of guilt, there is room, of course, for an entire range of intermediary states. Remorse, for instance, in the form of a sense of irritation at having failed, gnawing regret, resentment, anguish are bound to be poison to the psyche. Repentance is healthy and sane only when sealed with humility, faith and love. And it alone liberates, pacifies and restores lost equilibrium.

All priests are bound to come across anguished souls, a prey to a morbid sense of guilt, and they are bound by their very calling to try to deliver them by maintaining in them a delicate sense of sin—arousing it if need be. On that account, a description and comparison of the two states will not be superfluous.

Morbid guilt feelings can be traced to the most varied sources, like the other neuroses, of which they are frequently either a consequence or the cause, or possibly a principal manifestation.

The causes may be organic: a lesion, or any disease producing a weakening of the nervous system. Or they may be psychic, e.g. an emotional shock, intense fear, a setback, a bereavement; in short, any "accident" that profoundly affects the personality.

A psychic cause about which a great fuss has been made, since Freud, is what is called repression. Here we cannot attempt to explain so complex a theory in detail. But it went on and on evolving in its author's head, and remains very imprecise, arbitrary and absurd in many of its components, though it does none the less contain valuable discoveries.

For Freud, neuroses are due—often, not always—to the repression of the Libido, i.e. the sexual energy or instinct, which is supposed to constitute the original source and hence the explicit centre of all human activity. Repression is the unconscious rejection of manifestations of the Libido, when censured by an authority within us which Freud calls the Super-Ego, self-invested with the double function of judge and executioner. The form it takes is traceable either to the repression of sexual impulses of infantile origin, in particular the Œdipus complex, or to the whole series of parental, social and religious prohibitions that surround the child. Driven back into the unconscious, the urges inhibited by the Super-Ego continue to act darkly and disturbingly within the psyche. Hence the instigation of neuropathic states. Hence, too, the feeling of guilt that accompanies or engenders them.

Whatever may be said of Freud's exaggeration, over-simplification, and wrong-headedness, it would be foolish to underestimate the part played by repression in the formation of neurosis, and particularly of repression occurring during the very early years of life under the influence, no matter whether unconscious or deliberate, of "the children's first gods", i.e. their parents. We will return to this later.

One of the principal of Freud's errors is believing that a repression of instinctive urges is alone the source of neuroses. As a great French psychiatrist, Dr Baruk, has most ably pointed out,[1] it may be true that certain neuroses are consequent on the repression of instincts, notably sexual desires, but what Freud completely lost sight of is the dire consequences of repression of the *conscience*. "This repression has far more serious results than the repression of instincts, which is at least confined to the limited, individual field of neuropathic disturbances, not on the whole malignant ones. Whereas repression of conscience may determine not only serious psychoses but reactions of a kind to provoke veritable social catastrophes."

Facts are available to prove beyond doubt that it is not always repression of instinctive desires, but on the contrary, their fulfilment at the expense of the moral law, that causes deterioration of the personality. First the voice of conscience is stilled. Then the fault is committed. Then the feeling of true guilt is repressed. This double repression works havoc. Baruk cites a number of cases, among them the following. A director of a business was suddenly seized with intense hatred for an employee whom he wished to have dismissed. No valid proofs of misconduct were forthcoming. But the director denounced him with such violence that people concluded he must have done something terrible. Conflicting views rent the establishment and the trouble spread. The situation got more and more out of hand. Finally it emerged that a remark made by the employee had been repeated to the director: it referred to an irregularity of conduct on the part of the director, which he believed he had kept hidden and unperceived.

Finally, though one ought not to assume too readily, in dealing with guilt neuroses, that the cause may be supernatural or preternatural, the possibility should not be rejected

---

[1] Dr Baruk is Chief Medical Doctor of the Maison nationale de Charenton, Professor at the Medical Faculty in Paris, and the author of numerous works on psychiatry (see List of Books referred to at the end of this volume).

a priori. In certain cases, for example in the lives of some saints, very well-balanced people in other respects, a scrupulous condition might be seen as a trial sent from God. In other cases, the possibility of diabolical intervention is not to be excluded.

But normal guilt is the natural consequence of the sin. Conscience is well aware that it yielded, partially or wholly, to a temptation. And when the question of consent is not clear, conscience is aware of this too and knows what to do about it. The perspicacity of conscience varies in degree, of course. Increase of lucidity comes as one of the most important conquests of the moral life, on condition, we must repeat, that it never be separated from other elements of Christian morality, and that humble adhesion to Christ the Redeemer—without which one might well "lose heart".

The most usual manifestation of morbid guilt is anguish: in its acute form it is betrayed by facial expression, gesture, speech and general agitation; its less acute forms are anxiety, worry, a sense of insecurity. In normal guilt, so long as there is remorse only, there is also anguish. When remorse turns into contrition the anguish disappears, leaving simply an awareness of having disobeyed, together with regret, compunction, the assurance that the recovery of integration is possible, and hence—peace.

In morbid guilt, the patient has a feeling that some evil power is driving or threatening him, or else that a mysterious curse is laid on him. He feels an immense need of protection, and not finding it anywhere, he goes from doctor to doctor and from confessor to confessor. Sometimes he turns to anyone who happens to be there. In normal guilt, a man admits his responsibility, and if he seeks advice and support, it is of a kind suggested or prescribed by natural prudence or faith.

Morbid guilt often strikes an individual in his innermost

self, in his "holy of holies", in his most vital fibre: for a soldier, it is his honour; for a fighting man, his courage; for an honest citizen, his dignity; for a religious, his faith; for a young mother, her maternal affection; for a virgin, or a priest true to his vow of chastity, it is purity. But it often happens that the obsession conceals other aspects of moral life in which the patient behaves with a total lack of scruple. Normal people also frequently have their weakness, or flaw, or special danger-point; but they know it and are serious and calm about it. With no fuss or worry, they keep quietly in mind the need to be on their guard.

In morbid guilt, doubt has the upper hand: Is it a sin? Have I sinned?—an agonized question, provoking fastidious examinations of conscience, and all to no avail, for confusion grows; or leading to long-winded expatiations at confession and an endless chewing over the same problem. In normal guilt, an examination of conscience is feasible and good. Boldly done, it can be revealing and engender a progressive clarification of the conscience, tracking down not only acts but also intentions and even hidden motives.

In morbid guilt, it is not rare to find the patient trying to conjure the "fate" that threatens him, or fight to free himself from the grip of his obsession, indulging in various odd practices and superstitious rituals; he may seek for "signs" to restore his self-confidence, or commit acts of auto-punishment[1] or look for a scapegoat to whom to transfer his burden of culpability. But all his efforts are worse than useless and the patient remains a prey to his obsessions. Guilt then

---

[1] Some even nurse the idea of suicide, or actually commit suicide. In some cases the mechanism of auto-punishment plays its part unconsciously. An unmarried woman of thirty-five who involuntarily caught sight of her father's genitals, and did so again in nursing him, became blind. No organic cause could be found, and psycho-analysis was prescribed. This brought to light the scruple that had provoked the auto-punishment, and the girl regained her sight.

becomes a chronic and irreducible state. In normal guilt, on the contrary, a man complains of no one but himself, and if he submits to sanctions or imposes expiation on himself, it is in a spirit of reparation governed by his conscience's awareness of the misdeed done, and with the intention of curbing the tendencies underlying his faults. Hand in hand with repentance, expiation can liquidate the feeling of guilt, or more exactly, transform it into compunction, contrition, that is, a healthy sorrow for the fault once committed, now pardoned; and this can be the starting-point for more fervour in love, and a renewal of generosity. Culpability is here a more or less brief state of mind consequent on a real fault; it is a reducible state, that is, it can be transformed by means of repentance and confession.

In morbid guilt, the struggle with repressed urges seems desperate and doomed. The urges appear irresistible, and at the same time culpable. The patient lives perpetually exposed to imperious temptations. He confuses temptation and sinning. In normal guilt, the struggle with one's tendencies appears to be in order, even if it is not always successful. Conscience lives in the hope of resisting better and better, and diligently seeks out the means to do so, in all lucidity and sincerity. Temptation and sin are clearly distinguishable. If a man firmly resists temptation, he knows it and is aware of his innocence. And he knows if his complicity was partial and without full consent (venial sin), or if he was totally involved (grave sin if the occasion was grave).

In morbid guilt, any desire to do good is likely to melt away in due course, through the apparent impossibility of ever achieving it. Every set-back, whether real or imaginary, augments the sense of impotence. Finally, conduct is wholly governed by the sole notion of evil and the struggle with evil. It is thus purely negative and dominated by fear. At times, weary of fighting, the patient throws the entire moral law to the winds and plunges headlong into vice. But far from bringing relief, this would-be remedy only adds fuel to the fire. In normal guilt, a deliberate awareness of the good to be loved and pursued brings confidence that evil may be overcome. Each success increases this sense, so long as humility is also present. Conduct is regulated by the notion of good, and evolves under the governance of the values to which a man adheres, values which nourish his inward vision: God, Jesus Christ, neighbours, family, society, career, vocation. It is activated by love.

In morbid guilt, a man feels perpetually guilty, he always has a sense of insufficiency, indignity, disgust with himself. Suggestions of pardon, innocence, purity regained, are rejected. Confession does not seem to help. Religion, if he has any, is dominated by fear and an exclusive preoccupation with himself. The Gospel is taken as a collection of exactions and threats. God appears as an avenging power and nothing else. In normal guilt a man has the feeling that the moral life is something possible. He sees his own dangers and weaknesses but knows that with the help of God's grace, and with good will, and time on his side, good can be made to predominate at last; and in the meantime, till a more dependable stability is achieved, every victory is of value, even if there are not only victories. If he sins, he knows that sincere contrition and sacramental absolution renew a life down to the very roots, and he experiences a feeling of relief and innocence regained, with no misgivings. Confession is beneficial, liberating. Penance is accepted, understood and carried out as just reparation, and as a means of curbing and purifying natural urges; it is active participation in his own redemption. The sense of insufficiency and indignity experienced does not prevent the religious life from being lived in serenity, confidence and joy. And the religious life is a source of dynamism and interior unity. As for the Gospel, it is of course the book of sovereign love as well as sovereign demands. God is Love and Mercy, He is the Father, He is the Saviour come to save what was lost. Even if I sin seven times seventy-seven times, He is always ready to welcome me back as soon as I humbly turn to Him.

IV. THE PREVENTION OF MORBID GUILT

In the space at our disposal, it is not possible to consider all aspects of a problem of extreme delicacy: that of training consciences. A few summary remarks must suffice, dealing with the moral education of children under seven and the inculcating of a straightforward, sensitive and healthy conscience.

These are, in fact, the decisive years. Modern psychology and psycho-analysis stress the importance of a child's early life in the formation of the psyche, but not without indulging in quite a number of fanciful notions in the interpretation of the facts. However, it cannot be denied that the happy or unhappy development of a child is closely dependent on how those years are spent.

Many neuroses owe their origin to events occurring then, even if in certain cases they only come to light at an advanced age. Dr Paul Cossa tells of a man of fifty-eight who had suffered since he was fifty from an obsession with dirt. He could not sit down without first carefully wiping his seat all over, for it always appeared to him to be marked with numerous stains. In course of psycho-analysis it turned out that at the age of seven or eight the patient was the victim of a young aunt of a perverse turn of mind who had "interfered" with him, committing *fellatio*. All his sexual life had been affected by this incident. He was capable of normal sexual relations as a married man, but had a preference for *fellatio*, and not wanting to impose it on his wife, he sought other obliging partners without much care for their quality as people. Having revealed this to his doctor, the patient disappeared, reappearing three weeks later to say, "Doctor, I have been to confession and I have made a firm resolution to give up this habit. Doctor, I am cured." He was cured, and he remained so. Note the twofold source of origin of the neurosis: an unconscious one and a conscious one, the former without trace of real culpability (an incident in childhood), the latter constituted by a real sense of guilt, and the two overlapping.

Hence it is particularly important during that period to avoid anything that might exaggerate or distort the child's sense of guilt. As early moral training is almost exclusively in the hands of the parents, it is they whose education needs completing. It is regrettable how thoughtless and impulsive many parents are, even the better-educated ones. Clearly psycho-somatic heredity plays a great part in children's development. The blunders and mistakes of their early upbringing leave few traces on some of them, it is true, but there are others for whom a single mistake can have the most disastrous consequences. Great vigilance is needed in all cases.

Now let us run through a few important rules which people constantly need to be reminded of, because they are constantly ignored or infringed.

(1) We must avoid judging a child's actions as though he possessed our adult awareness and our scale of values; exaggerating his faults, or scolding and punishing him excessively, which puts his conscience out of focus. We knew a working man of forty who suffered from a serious anxiety neurosis with almost complete inhibition of the power to communicate ideas or feelings. Once, as a small boy of six or seven, he had stolen a watch from home and bartered it for a much-coveted spinning-top. It is probable that the violent and disproportionate reprimand of his father on

discovering the misdeed was the origin of the neurosis that poisoned his whole life. Of course a child has to be taught not to lie and steal, but it is very wrong to measure his intentions and his larceny by the standards of an adult conscience.

(2) Careless things done by a child, like breaking a flower vase or tearing his clothes or accidentally wetting his bed, should not be treated on the same level as faults for which he is responsible. First, because it distorts his conscience. A child (like many adults, sad to say) is already all too inclined to measure the enormity of his fault by the amount of visible damage done, rather than by his sense of responsibility. In the eyes of many parents, "it is more serious for a child to break a dozen plates in trying to be helpful, than a single saucer in playing a practical joke", as Berge has rightly pointed out.

In the second place, complexes very harmful for his growth and development may result. Arthus cites the case of a girl of twenty-one who was greatly distressed because nearly every night enuresis occurred. As a child she had endured appalling punishments on account of it, chiefly shaming ones, which had not had the smallest effect, apart from draining her of every ounce of self-confidence by afflicting her with a tenacious inferiority complex.

Finally, a child has a feeling for the difference between what he did out of naughtiness and what he did not do "on purpose". He is extremely sensitive to injustice, which can provoke the gravest psychic disturbances; and resentment, especially, can do the more harm for being carefully dissimulated or even unconsciously repressed.

(3) While encouraging a child's efforts to be tidy and clean, silent, quiet, polite, his parents should avoid putting it to him as part of his duty to God: they can appeal to the obedience due to parents, or to convention. We have no right to mix

God with our rules and regulations for good manners and civilized behaviour. The same could be said of certain rules for "good manners" in church. Dalto tells the story of a little girl of ten who underwent a crisis of anxious distress before her First Communion, because she was afraid of biting the Host by mistake, and of hurting "little Jesus", making Him bleed—and then going to Hell. That is what they had been told at the Catechism class, she declared. She could not be calmed down till she had been made to understand that it was just the teacher's way of putting things, like when they tell your whole row to stand up, or genuflect; that is, it was just a matter of deference due, and no serious sin was involved by not doing it right.

It is extremely dangerous for parents to invoke God to cover an injustice or to support an act of repression which, erroneously or not, might be registered as an injustice by the child. "Even if parents act unjustly, human injustice never kills a child spiritually, unless the profile of those inflicting the wound is projected on to the shadow of God."

(4) Then there is the bogey-man—not everywhere extinct, unfortunately. Children are still sometimes threatened with horrible chastisements, and death and hell, if they go on with their "bad ways". "If you're not good I'll call the policeman"—or the priest, as a kind of policeman to punish small delinquents. Sometimes spirits run too high and someone gets hurt, following an act of disobedience; and then they are told that God is punishing them. In some countries, in the humbler city homes (and also in rural districts), we find children of a cringing docility through over-strict training in proper behaviour, all in the name of a God who sees everything and "punishes". It is terrible to hear Christian mothers say to their children, "Jesus has punished you"—when they have merely run wild or disobeyed well-intentioned parental injunctions.

Such methods are of no use at all in developing a child's conscience. This has to be ruled by love of good and not fear of evil and dread of punishment, which merely leave a child defenceless and impotent under the rule of a rigid and unreasonable Super-Ego. "In the name of 'education' many things are done to children with the sole purpose, it would seem, of making them think they are surrounded by fearful, threatening powers that peer into their secret heart and impose heavy penalties for the least sign of independence" (Berge).

Thus the ground is prepared for the seeds of anxiety to take root and grow. Or in other cases the outcome of it all will be scepticism. As the child discovers the emptiness of the threats showered down on his head, he comes to consider all the entities involved to be illusory, including God whom he only knew as one of them. In some cases a certain *erotic* tinge is found: "It is not rare to come across people who take a kind of pleasure in their scruples and remorse and obsessions, in short, in all the torments inflicted by their beloved tyrant" (Berge). Anyone who has had to do with victims of anguish or scrupulosity may have observed how sometimes a sort of masochism accompanies the neuropathic state. To quote Berge again: "It is a matter of conjecture whether one of the essential characteristics of pathological culpability does not reside in the sly pleasure taken in it."

(5) One very delicate and crucial section of children's upbringing is education in modesty and purity. The tremendous influence of Freud and psycho-analysis in the sexual interpretation of phenomena of infantile life is common knowledge. Most psychologists nowadays distinguish four or five overlapping phases in the "sexual" evolution of early infancy, namely:

(*i*) The "oral" phase, marked by inordinate satisfaction in sucking the breast or its substitute; (*ii*) the "anal" phase, characterized by inordinate satisfaction in the act of excretion and interest in the result; (*iii*) the "genital" phase, during which the child grows interested in his sex and tries to touch himself in play; (*iv*) the "narcissic" phase, when the child displays interest in the whole of the body; (*v*) the hetero-sexual phase, when he becomes aware of the differentiation of the sexes; this is the stage when the famous Œdipus complex becomes manifest.

These various phases are supposed to be closely linked to the child's affective life, and on their issue, wise or otherwise, the adult psyche is said to depend: there will be equilibrium, or there will be disturbance due to complexes or neuroses.

There is no time to discuss these propositions here; but one thing is certain, when a child starts exploring his genitals he ought to be stopped, just as in any other "bad habits", like sucking his thumb or his pillowslip, or putting dirt into his mouth. Not with fierce looks or scolding fingers, nor with threats. In earliest infancy, his hand should merely be moved away, gently, but firmly enough for the intention to be clear. Later on he can be told that "well-behaved children don't do that". Cleanliness can be referred to, but care must be taken in every case, for it is a pity when a child's first inkling of sexual life is of something supposedly dirty. What should form in his mind is not a sense of shame, but one of respect.

By invoking good manners, one can gradually teach a child modesty. Up to the age of five or six, it is more advis-able to let children dress, undress and wash together.[1] They get to know the difference between the sexes without being affected by it. Then comes the time to persuade them to

[1] On the other hand they must carefully be shielded from seeing the nudity of grown-ups, even those nearest to them. Writers on the subject insist that a child should be given a room apart from his parents as early as possible.

change to less free-and-easy ways. If it is given out, casually, that as a rule, once they no longer need help or supervision, "people are best left alone" to do their washing and dressing, it ought not to be too difficult to pass imperceptibly from behaviour good enough for "little folk" to the behaviour commonly observed by the "grown-ups" of the family (Berge).

With regard to sex, a child's curiosity awakens at a very early stage. Freud asserts that it sometimes appears before the third year. De Greeff states that from three or four years of age onwards, sexual curiosity, or at least an aptitude for it, is very evident. Generally speaking, the discovery of the difference between boys and girls will give rise to questions, and.so will other family occurrences. Any show of surprise is to be avoided and no embarrassment should be felt: a child quickly knows when his questions are unwelcome. He may pretend not to care and keep them to himself, and this is a repression that may do harm. It is of course still more important not to scold him or laugh at him, or tell him lies. There is only one good method for dealing with a child's questions: and that is, give him a true answer in the most natural way possible, as suitable for his age.

A word about the Œdipus complex. Briefly, it consists for a boy in becoming inordinately attached to his mother, with a feeling of aggression and fear, tinged with a sense of guilt, towards his father whom he takes for his rival. For a girl the problem is supposed to be different: it is how to give expression to her preference for her father without becoming estranged from the mother whom she still needs so badly.

Everyone is aware of the capital part played by the Œdipus complex in Freud's psychological system. For a great number of psychologists it has become a veritable axiom. Yet, probably, in many cases, it does not exist at all, or merely consists in the normal attitude that any human being spontaneously adopts towards other people, whether of the opposite sex or of his own. But then it is no longer a complex. Where it does exist, it is probably due to blundering on the part of father or mother; the father treating his son roughly, or ironically, or with indifference, and letting his preference for his daughter show too much; and the mother doting on her son, with a touch of jealousy that makes her find her daughter's bursts of affection for her father a little trying.

Whether nature or the parents are responsible for its existence, the Œdipus complex needs skilful handling if psychic disasters are to be avoided later on. It happens naturally, if the parents are and appear to be closely united, and refrain from putting the silly question, "Which do you love most?" and both showing equal love for sons and daughters; and on family occasions, turn and turn about, mother and all the children, father and all the children, can unite to work out secret plans for a special show of affection to the other partner.

The greatest danger threatening a child is lack of understanding between his parents, and the temptation that besets each of them to seek compensation in the child. Many forsaken wives are inclined to concentrate all their affection on their small boy, and to monopolize his affection, whereas it ought to go out to other objects as well. Then the feminine ideal that the boy develops is too close to the maternal ideal. The result may later on be total impotence, or impotence solely in relation to his wife, whom he loves indeed but treats as a remote divinity. There is indubitable evidence in his posthumous work, *Et nunc manet in te*, that this was André Gide's case.

Sometimes, hoping to arouse in her son a very splendid ideal of purity, a devout mother will provoke a feeling of disgust and dread towards sexuality, even in a boy's early childhood. Later on she will put him excessively on his guard in regard to girls and women instead of gradually revealing to him how great and grave a thing love is. Then it may happen that the young man will feel no attraction at all for girls, but in compensation feel drawn to boys. The most legitimate marriage-tie will seem to him to be laid under an interdict, whereas homosexuality will appear the lesser vice, or even something perfectly natural. According to those who have studied the matter, eighty per cent of homosexual cases can be traced to a mother's mistakes.

(6) Whatever field of morality may be involved, whether obedience, or justice, or modesty, or charity, a child's efforts should be stimulated by a love of good and of God, and not by fear and punishment. This does not mean that punishment should never be inflicted. Parents need to be warned as to the danger of repeated threats, but the imposition of punishment in given cases is a different matter. De Greeff gives a fine instance of a correction judiciously administered in a particularly difficult case. He also says that hell should never be mentioned to children under five, and that it is wholly superfluous to inculcate fear of chastisement.

In replying to a child's questions, it is very important that those concerned should sow in his mind an accurate picture of the world, as a world on which neither he nor they can have any influence, a world depending on a will that no one can tamper with. Without being frightening at all, parents need to teach their child to obey the "angel of light" that dwells within him and is the best part of him: and to follow his more generous ideas, for love of his parents as well as love of other people, and for love of Jesus most of all, who can see everything, understand everything, and loves little children.

In short, the infantile guilt feeling, that exists spontaneously in a child and is often made more burdensome through mistakes committed in his vicinity, needs guiding towards a sense of personal responsibility. A child should have a true, healthy awareness of his own mistakes and faults, and be encouraged to persevere in his efforts to achieve goodness in all freedom of spirit; and this is done by love. "What should emerge is a clear awareness of the value of things. To that end, parents, each of them, need to begin by themselves discriminating distinctly between their own legitimate personal demands (or the rules and regulations they are entitled to lay down) and the exalted laws whose universal application they proclaim best by being the first to submit to them. The result will be, no longer a helpless feeling of guilt, but a sense of responsibility for one's own actions, implying that one is conscious of having intended them, instead of passing through life like a Kafka character, fearful but uncomprehending" (Berge).

Appendix

COLLABORATION BETWEEN PRIESTS AND DOCTORS

Priests and doctors alike often come across neurotic psyches and they ought to combine their efforts to heal or at least alleviate them. But unfortunately an attitude of great distrust still prevails between them, as a rule. Let us consider the reasons for this.

Moralists have the impression that doctors put too much trust in therapeutic and physiological methods. The ones who venture into the field of psycho-therapy are very rare. They find doctors often misconstrue an appeal to moral, social, spiritual or religious values, and even pour scorn on it. It is not very unusual to find a doctor has recommended practices in the sexual sphere that are directly contrary to morality. Sometimes the impression is given that even for Christian doctors, notions of conscience, morality, freedom, will, culpability, religion, are *practically* ignored in their view of a patient's world. There is no need to bring Freud into it with his system of turning all the higher values—art, morality, religion—into sublimated products of the Libido, creations of the Super-Ego. Hesnard makes a praiseworthy attempt to distinguish between science and psychology on the one hand, and metaphysics on the other. Yet at the end of his book he plunges headlong into a discussion on the moral problem with most regrettable results. After deploring the moralists' distrust of science when they could make such good use of its findings, he adds:

"We incline to the idea that the moralists' failure is principally due to the fact that they deign to turn to science only when searching for rather vague information, and not for what it can really offer them.

"We have been struck with admiration by the sincere, lyrical panegyrics of the Good by authors of text-books on Morality. But does this conscientious and splendid definition of the moral Ideal, and the declaration that morality, the superb creation of man aspiring to perfection, is like a 'metaphysics in process', *practically speaking* advance us in the least degree? Has this theoretical morality penetrated into the masses, influenced the infantile sadistic atmosphere of schools and play-time. . . . For all the hymning through the centuries of what man ought to be . . . is humanity any the better, any less engaged in violence, less scornful of the life of its members, less full of hatred? . . . Religious morality and philosophical morality have therefore failed. . . .

"The science of sociology and of human customs has somewhat tempered their appetite for sterile speculation on the Good as such." From psychology they have merely gained "a horrified impression of the brutality and ugliness of the depths of the human being. A renewal of the Christian tradition of the basic perversion of human nature. . . .

"But the moralists ought to have wondered how morality could issue from basically 'immoral' attitudes. And tried to account for the mysterious gulf that separates original sin from the marvellous ideal which they try to induce man to cultivate. They should have tried to trace the stages of that strange mutation linking what is immoral to what is holy through the average ethical man, the only individual of any interest for those who prefer action to vain speculation. . . .

"If humanity does not disappear, as seems possible at the moment, in a collective suicide committed by degrees, the day will doubtless come when, having at last learnt to bring young people up away from Sin and in genuine social contact, it will be composed of an active majority of individuals whose need for strong action will be adapted to collective life and canalized in athletics, emulation, and mutual assistance. Then at last it will be possible to prescribe a theoretical morality, which will have to be, above all, a *Morality without sin*, that is to say, a Morality which will be, above all, a perfected Ethic. Then the psychiatrist will deal with all that the present Morality of Sin has handled so badly, and particularly all that has to do with auto-erotic sexuality, leaving to the moralist, by way of sexual morality, merely what concerns the social relations of the sexes. As for the Christian precept, theoretically wonderful but with no effect on the masses, to forgive wrongs and to love your enemy, it shall give place to the realizable precept of respect for the human person, down to the necessary practice of protecting society by eliminating from communal life (though not as punishment) dangerous non-civic and anti-social individuals. Thus Morality, now become universal, founded not on general science or scientism but on the *experimental science of moral conduct*, will be in conformity with the human condition, that is to say, evident and useful. By rational conditioning of human conduct, you would obtain from all of mankind what the mystics obtain from a few, namely, *non-violence* in human relations.

"By freeing the individual of those mystical fears of a bygone age, experimental science will return him to his social task."

It is pages like those, with all their naïveté and pretentiousness, that make the moralists distrustful of men of science.

Fortunately, there are also others with a more exact notion of the limitations of experimental science, who admit the part played by conscience, the Christian conception of sin, and a sincerely religious life, in giving equilibrium to the human personality and healing or at least alleviating neuropathic states.

We mentioned Dr Baruk, who works in France—a practising Jew. He came to realize that even in lunatics there subsists an important residue of conscience, and therefore gives moral treatment a privileged place in the treatment of neuroses and psychoses.

In Switzerland, Dr Tournier is well known for the books in which he tells of his psychotherapeutic work. His field is mainly among patients afflicted with relatively light neuroses, the outcome of loneliness, resentment, feelings of revenge, exaggerated independence, incapacity to accept trials, and so on. A sincere Protestant, Dr Tournier makes no bones about proposing for his patients a "soul cure", that is, recollection, examination of conscience, forgiveness, confession, prayer, submission to reality and to God's will. His books need refocusing a little, but they contain psychological views without scientific pretensions, and deal with the kind of cases most currently met with in our ministry.

As for the moralists, Hesnard is right to regret that hitherto they have shown too little interest in scientific discoveries, especially those of psychology. Their attitude has now begun slowly to evolve. But any attention they may devote to these problems must not be allowed to distract them from dealing, as in the past, with conscience, intrinsic good, sin, redemption, and persuading men to pursue the only ideals that can help them to outgrow instinctive life and give primacy to spiritual things within them.

Healthy psyches and neurotic psyches alike must be orientated and induced to come to terms with true values: work, society, family, neighbours and God. They can thus be diverted from the fundamental egocentricity which exists in all men and is found in an exacerbated state in all morbid conditions. And even in cases where life is hard to bear, it will at least bear fruit. Very often there will be evident improvement in the most damaged psyche. As Simone Weill wrote, "In people who love God, the glands do not function in the same way as in others; the love of God being, of course, the cause and not the effect of this difference". St Paul's heartening words might be interpreted in the same way: "*Diligentibus Deum omnia cooperantur in bonum* . . ."[1] And we shall not forget that St Augustine added, "*Etiam peccata*".

[1] Rom. viii. 28.

IV

PRIESTS AND RELIGIOUS AS TEACHERS

By Abbé Louis Fourneau

Inspector of Primary Schools, Namur

THE teacher who wants a good return for his efforts must ask himself some questions.

What exactly happens when he talks to his class? He knows roughly what goes on in his own mind—but what about his pupils'?—Some lessons have disappointing results, while others are very successful. What accounts for it? As teachers, it is always possible that we do not pay sufficient attention to the complexity of the mental factors involved, and have hitherto taken too simplified a view and worked on too simple a scheme. *A priori* we do not know, and this is not a problem to be solved by reflection alone. Positive psychology has a good deal to tell us about the relations between teacher and taught.

Granted the problem cannot be solved by logical argument. A teacher wanting to do his job well can work out a scheme in his mind that only needs producing in proper sequence to be effective—or so he imagines. The pupil merely has to take what he is given, bit by bit, in the right order, and piece it all together in his mind, with no gaps. Well, the pupil who cannot do it is lazy and stupid. Or he is not up to it physically. Or he could, but won't. Or with the best will in the world he just hasn't the brains for it. The individual psychology of his pupils is not what interests the teacher, he is concerned with a standard pupil, whom he supposes to be motivated by a logical system similar to that of an adult. In broad outline, that is still the attitude of not a few teachers who have never found leisure to peruse the pages of text-books of modern psychology. After all, they work according to honoured tradition, on methods deemed infallible—and they are not without their quota of laziness.

Today, everyone knows that things are not like that at all. Even in fields as "clear" as mathematical reasoning, the processes of thought are not those of traditional logic. Everyone knows, too, that in the search for truth man's emotions and instincts are engaged as well as his mind, which you have no right to try to cut off from the rest of the psyche on pretext of being clear and properly pedagogical. Let us see what contemporary psychology can do for us.

We want to discover how to teach well. A solution to the problem with which we will have nothing to do consists in deducing from a very summary form of traditional philosophical psychology, pedagogical applications for use in and out of season. This procedure, current in certain training colleges thirty years ago, has still not completely vanished from the curriculum. An example will show why it is indefensible.

We are told there is nothing in the intelligence that has not come there via the senses; and in consequence, it is courting disaster not to make teaching intuitive. As the senses have to play their part for an idea to take shape in a child's mind, we need only provide a series of colourful pictures and our teaching will automatically benefit. Let things be seen, show your class pictures and films, and the budding idea will be the richer for it.

That is only partially right. First, it is not clear what philosophical psychology is in evidence, though it may be the one declaring man to be an entity, and his knowledge an entity too, so that even the highest form of thought remains that of a man immersed in a world of sense, and always retains some trace of it. Written words are of the senses, so are spoken words, so are the teacher's movements and the whole setting of the lesson. Should you wish to remove this element, there would be no more teacher, no more words uttered, no more classroom, no more lessons or books, and the problem would not arise. Philosophical reflection on the subject of human knowledge does not, in fact, teach us whether a history lesson showing a film is preferable to the history lesson without a film. Only experience can tell, and direct experiment; then the results can be collated and compared by different groups of pupils, one taught with films in regular use, the other going on receiving traditional lessons from a no less traditional teacher. The value of a method can be judged by the results obtained. But it is unwise to go too far, concluding that the more room is made for intuition, the better the results will be. Experience shows nothing of the sort; it simply demonstrates that in certain conditions certain results are obtainable. Which means we shall have to take a more modest view of our potentialities. But in teaching, as elsewhere, it is high time we did.

I. THE QUEST FOR TRUTH

What we have to transmit to our children is not so much material, not a certain baggage of facts; still less is it our job to shove it into them willy-nilly, while all they need do is to sit there passively, regardless of the world around them— that of the senses or otherwise.

Far from it. They are young people in full process of growth, with everything in them on the *qui-vive*. It is absurd to suppose a system can be invented by which facts about the material world and the world of ideas can be inserted into their minds with the help of the senses, their own part being merely to ratify what is done in all docility. That is not how things work. Boys and girls are out in search of truth, and their energies are engaged in the search, even though they cannot always know what it is they want. But there exists in them—as in all of us—a keen need to be adapted to the world in which they are immersed. In our day, this fact receives more attention than it did formerly, and the main instrument of adaptation is held to be the intelligence. Instinct is not enough, and we know it: among our urges there are universal aspirations which instinct with its closed doors cannot satisfy; there are adaptations which the immediacy of instinct will never be able to affect. In fact, every intellectual act can be seen, from this angle, as the answer to a question, or the remedy to a lack of adaptation (taking adaptation in the broadest sense of the word). People want to know or assimilate something, they want to "comprehend" and "grasp" it. All the great problems of mankind can be reduced to the fact that one must live—life embracing everything from the need to eat to the necessity of contemplation. We have to live, and we try to nourish our life; we have to know, love, comprehend: that is what underlies our mental activity. We do well not to forget it, so as not to force drink on someone who is not thirsty. For the great thing is to be aware of what is going on. A student has a real thirst to be quenched, and that is our concern—or we are merely wasting our time on problems that do not arise.

In fact, the wise teacher has a keen awareness of his pupils. His teaching is not a one-sided matter of doling out information. The child sees a problem from his own point of view. The question is, is he ready to take in what he is being taught? Does previous work, careful teaching, personal tastes, the desire to get on, make him want to make the most of the lesson? Does he show any interest in what is said and done in class? Or is he merely wondering how soon he can escape?

It is frankly insufficient for us to have only our own rather hazy ideas on the value of compulsory intellectual discipline; their response is equally important, and for this to occur, they must be somehow made aware of the connection between their own urgent vitality and the work required of them. This does not at all mean that concrete motives must be found for everything, with practical applications in view all the time—rather difficult in the case of a Latin prose or a mathematical proof. It is in fact absurd. But in the primary schools there is a tendency to give impetus to a child's capacity to learn by showing what practical use it can have. Hundreds of articles have appeared on this subject and a great deal of nonsense has been written. It may be just possible, though rather far-fetched, to justify the learning of arithmetic by the need to go shopping, but no such claims can be made for knowing the distance of stars or the causes of the Hundred Years War. But when we are told how necessary it is for a teacher to hold the attention of his class, it is something of the same kind that is meant: for he needs to make the problem present to their minds, in all its complexity, so that they feel challenged to make the effort required of them to solve it. This is not to turn teaching into a game, or to sugar the pill, it is letting boys and girls know what is involved and winning their support, that is to say, their consent to making the effort.

Even in an elementary catechism class, where the application of psychology may seem out of place, the same thing holds. Consider the two methods: one consists of explanations based on the passage the children are learning; the other starts from people and things. In the first, the children learn a list of the Sacraments, then they take each one in detail, matter, form, effects, and the rest of it: starting from the catechism itself and learning nothing but catechism. The teacher is not concerned with the child's attitude. But how different the approach is when we keep to Jesus Christ Himself, alive and present to the children, who know who He is and how He comes to save us, to listen to our troubles and care for our needs. You come to the catechism in the long run. But meantime, you have followed the way of our Lord's teaching. He started from the people's own aspirations. He made the problem apparent—think of how He revealed the Holy Trinity (the Father speaking, and sending down the Holy Spirit); think of the Manna in the desert, and what the cherished memory of it meant to the Jews; then the multiplication of the loaves, and the talk that followed but was not understood—and the difficulties all this created for men of good will.

But until recently, what a mess our primary schools made of it all.

II. THE INTELLIGENCE AND ITS MULTIPLE ASPECTS

A first-year student-trainee begins to study individual psychology and discovers that the intelligence can be measured. He learns to measure children's mental development. He has a rather summary knowledge of psychological factors, and has to understand as best he may. In fact, he feels rather uncomfortable about it. He, together with large numbers of other people, thought the intelligence was an undifferentiated but well-defined capacity, and now he finds that measurements of mental development involve tests which seem to have very little reference to what he is on the look-out for; for all they consist in is, repeating numbers, drawing from memory, reconstructing a puzzle, giving the meaning of a word, explaining things by their common use. What he had in mind was how to do a sum or parse a sentence or write a composition, and instead of that he is presented with a series of numbers, a box to be opened, shapes to fit together. He feels quite at sea. True, the subject is mental development, not just intelligence as such, which may account for his bewilderment. He is set to watch children in a nursery school. He comes on a small boy who is able to continue a pattern begun on the board (two yellow squares, one blue one), and who notices that the flags at the windows on the left fall to the right, while the one on the right falls to the left. That small boy is said to be "intelligent". His little neighbour cannot yet arrange things in order of size, and at five cannot distinguish between yellow and orange. So the student's verdict is, "this child is not intelligent", and the teacher concurs. But his previous ideas about intelligence are neither here nor there. On further enquiry, he learns that intellectual capacity awakens very early in life, at the nursery-school stage, before reason is present; and that sets him thinking. Why not, he ponders, if the men we consider intelligent are in fact those who succeed in concrete tasks. If it is all connected together, then there is no reason, of course, why a man's intelligence and a child's should only come into evidence through the ordinary run of school tests, like grammar, translation, or geometry. People's other ways of expressing themselves might form equally good tests, valid for the whole of a lifetime. Therefore our mania for expecting intelligence to manifest itself along logical lines and in scholarship rather than other ways may not be wholly justifiable. There are so many types of intelligence that it is extremely doubtful whether I have any right to judge on the results of one type of tests only.

That is a line of thought which we need to pursue much further than we do. Intelligence tests are numerous and diverse, not all equally valid or equally deserving of our confidence. But all aim at giving us a concrete view of the intelligent human being's reactions to a challenge, showing what he is capable of and which of many different tests are the ones he can do. We are much too prone to judge others on insufficient evidence, even committing ourselves to a final opinion when a child has merely taken tests of a scholastic nature that do not touch real life at all—"I give him 7 for intelligence". More modesty on our part would be pleasing, and we might have expressed our view differently: "On his answers to the questions set he deserves 7." For all we know, the child's intelligence may have hidden wealth stowed away, only valid in other fields.

One of the merits of individual psychology is that it draws our attention to this aspect of the problem and reduces the teacher's sense of omniscience to sizeable proportions: nowadays he dare not think he knows all about a boy when he has only just begun to watch him at work.

Another great advantage is that it restores our confidence. Teachers sometimes tend to despair of the children in their charge, but this is simply because they do not know them properly. And they do not know them because they were not capable of studying them usefully, because the criteria at their disposal were frankly insufficient. Were we to give our minds to the subject, we should discover how much harm is done by our errors of judgment, and admit that more guarantees are needed: the child requires much patient loving observation; our scrutiny should be made in the light of scientific tests, and our conclusions should only be drawn after good evidence has been obtained. Then there would undoubtedly be fewer misfits, and hence, fewer of life's failures.

We could also hope for more consideration for forms of intelligence that do not fit our mental categories and are not apt for fluent verbal expression or logical abstraction. If intelligence is an aptitude for solving problems, it is bound to vary according to the nature of the problems proposed to it. As Henri Piéron remarks:

"An engineer busy assembling the parts of a machine, an explorer finding his way through unknown country, a director engaged in resolving the difficulties of handling a heterogeneous group of employees, a politician haranguing a meeting, a mathematician unravelling a symbolical deduction, a physicist pursuing the cause of a phenomenon, a philosopher speculating on abstract concepts, an architect drawing a ground plan in accordance with given requirements and given conditions, a musician composing a symphony, and a sculptor carving a statue out of a piece of stone are all showing intelligence, but of a specialized and definitely non-interchangeable kind."

We pounce on what appears to be a privileged form of intelligence in a child and try to give it every chance—but again we may be wrong. For these so-called privileged intelligences are not psychologically verifiable: it is only from a sociological angle that they can be appreciated.

III. GROUP TEACHING AND INDIVIDUAL DIFFERENCES

We are not the first generation of teachers to note that children differ greatly in weight, size and character as well as intellectual capacity. There have always been the gifted and the rest, the difference being mainly a quantitative one. During the last forty years, research has dwelt on the qualitative differences between individuals: discovering not so much whether a child reaches average mental development for his age, as what there is to distinguish him from the others. An analysis is made of his capacity, his aptitudes in all conceivable directions, from purely sensory and sensor-motory aptitudes to the highest capacities known—not by-passing power of concentration. The value of the information obtained was immediately clear, for now, in school and vocational guidance, it is possible to provide candidates with indications and counter-indications based on well-tried tests, and not merely on impressions or statements made by themselves or their parents. Now that vocational guidance has come to be accepted by parents, educational authorities, industrial management and civil administration, it is high time that all teachers appreciated the possibility, and in fact the urgency, of an effective orientation during school years. Too many young people make a false start by being forced to undergo a course of study deemed to be the appropriate one for their social standing, regardless of other considerations. No one paused to wonder whether they could stand the pace, or whether they would not do better at something completely different.

There is one more point. As character-study advances, it becomes increasingly clear that human intelligence is a sort of vested interest or property that is influenced by character and can help to characterize a person.

In so far as it is a human activity, every act of the intelligence manifests the influence of character. Likewise, every type of character is partly defined by intellectual features of its own. Education in common, with children of different characters coming together in a classroom, serves to maintain and even to stress the various intellectual types. It happens even when all the children are treated alike, regardless of their different aptitudes, when one might have expected more of a levelling influence. But education is never an all-sufficing element of functional development. Far be it from us to put all men, all young people, through the same mould; in fact we must eschew the illusion of the general efficacy of a given method, or given practices, for all alike. The truth is, as we might suspect, much more complex.

A true educationalist cannot help remembering it, and has no right to ignore it. Each man's vocation is, as Le Senne put it so aptly, a compromise between what his character will allow him to become and the challenge of a given value; while the teacher's efforts can help him to discover and desire the latter, they cannot change character. It is not due to the teacher that a boy has an aptitude for certain subjects, all he can do is to respect it. Clearly, an education going against the grain of natural aptitudes will end in failure, except in the case of a particularly strong character.

You may like team-work in your class. Then each boy's character has to be considered in turn. The colourless, apathetic ones may greatly gain by contact with the quick-witted and be swept along in their wake; the highly-strung are helped by the perseverance and support of the team, the phlegmatic and the fiery show no inclination for being towed and prefer to get along on their own, which they often do very well. If they join a team, it will be as guides and pathfinders.

The same situation arises with certain procedures introduced in heavy doses into primary education and which tend to infiltrate into sections of secondary education. I refer to methods such as directed observation, investigations, reconstruction of the immediate neighbourhood and its ramifications, which are eminently suitable for extroverted children, who delight in them and do well; but are less valid for the reflective ones and the thinkers.

Indeed, there is no ready-made recipe for intellectual education: those who thought there was were mistaken. They were mistaken when they thought that practice was capable of producing a certain type of reflection and a way of thinking and judging; it is only superficially true, and only in the case of lessons learnt by rote at the cost of more vital and varied educational possibilities that would take congenital aptitudes into account. The loss incurred is a loss to the whole community. The initial mistake was, to claim that the mind can be trained, in some mysterious way, by a categorical set of studies, for all alike. With the result that those to whom they did not appeal fell by the wayside.

Teachers will be wise to think this over; it is well worth

while. No one form of study is suitable for all and sundry, no one exercise is valid for all minds: each individual has his own particular path to take, a path traced by his Creator and inscribed in his psyche as in his body. And it is only by following that path that he will become a person who can render to society what it has a right to expect of him.

That being so, why do we not squarely face the possibility of abandoning group teaching so as to let each child go along at his own pace and take his chance? It has been considered, and the "individual" school, with teaching based on individual aptitude, has been extolled. And at least in places where the new system is tried out pretty thoroughly, it alters the whole running of a class. The children work in silence, each pursuing his own study, a different one from his neighbour's. The teacher becomes a guide: instead of giving lessons to a group and setting exercises arising out of his lessons, he simply gives the children relevant information and helps them, correcting their answers to questions set individually, merely making sure that the syllabus is covered and the subject grasped and assimilated. One child is slower than another, one will want to spend longer on a piece of work that caught his imagination before going on to something else: all this is admissible. Is it not, indeed, the way we work ourselves? A boy can go ahead in one subject and be backward in another: in fact, it is the boys themselves who set the pace, and we adapt ourselves to them, instead of requiring them to adapt themselves to the teacher.

We may think what we like of the advantages and disadvantages of individualization, and we may prefer to use it only in very moderate amounts; but that, at the moment, is beside the point. We were merely observing how individual psychology, in stressing the differences between children in a class, does confront the teacher with certain problems. They cannot be ignored, and solutions have to be found. In fact, it looks as though some children's efforts to adapt themselves to a grammar school course, for instance, is sheer waste of their time. Better guidance at the beginning would have directed them towards a more suitable course, and inspired them with confidence to tackle it. For these young people are neither dunces nor duffers: but their education at a given stage was not of the right kind; that is all.

IV.　PLAY

During the last fifty years, many different accounts have been written of children's play, in all its different phases, from the smallest child waving his arms and legs because he needs movement, to the complicated social games with elaborate rules of older children. Here we see a child wanting to grow up quickly and playing at "Daddy", and there, schoolboys finding in competitive athletics an outlet for their young energies and a means of expressing their personalities.

This is not the place to describe forms of play, nor to take sides in an argument. But the subject has been amply studied and we are not entitled to regard play-time solely as relaxation, as though it were not commonly known that there is more to it than that. Playing is immensely important for the small child, for that is how he grows up, and he is extremely serious about it. And the word "play" ought never to be used in a pejorative sense, though I can think of certain colleagues of mine who find it comical to be expected to take an interest in nursery-school play. After all, we are the grown-ups and we know best—or do we? We have not studied the subject, but we know all about children. The poor school inspector is almost to be pitied for his professional bias, making him bother about such novelties. Whereas in reality, what a small child is doing may be much more serious than the solemn things that fill a grave and preoccupied gentle-

man's life. "I'm in earnest, I am", said the men to the Little
Prince in Saint-Exupéry's tale.

V. LEARNING

Here is a scene familiar to every teacher: children bent over a
sheet of paper covered with figures and diagrams, and
fidgeting because the solution doesn't "come". Some fumble
and embark on series of sums with no idea of what they are
about; others gaze at their rough diagrams, waiting for the
moment when light will dawn and the missing link be found;
suddenly they "see" and their faces light up: they've grasped
the problem. We watch beginners in Latin painfully trans-
lating word for word, without pausing a moment to try to
get hold of the general meaning of the passage, even if only
sketchily.

On this kind of learning some very interesting study has
been done in the last thirty years. We discover that there
are long underground channels along which work goes on
secretly, so that often the answer itself springs suddenly into
the mind—always supposing it is a mind able to grasp it. But
other ways are well known and well marked out, with the
goal in view: thus systematic research, with an hypothesis
that has to be verified and criticized. So it is, on the face of it,
a little too simple to tell our boys and girls to "go on trying"
and to "exert themselves". As though there were no real
problem at all.

In arithmetic (and more so in geometry), the link between
the data and the solution is not known and cannot be known
by means of reasoning: more than patience is needed to solve
the problem. For what we do not know is, which of the
various processes is applicable. Shall it be multiplication or
division, and why one rather than the other? Should a parallel
be drawn, should angles be compared, or not? We do not

know, and in principle there is no method that can tell us. We have to "see", and that is the whole problem. Among our pupils there is always one or more who does not "see" and never will see. If he can do arithmetic, it is because, in order to pass an examination, he has learnt how questions tend to group around certain types: once you know how the typical problem works, you can do the rest. No more can be asked of him than that. If the examination sets new problems, this candidate is hopelessly at sea.

But the others do surely deserve an apprenticeship in research methods. How can it be useful for a child to spend hours on composition when he has not yet grasped the structure of the sentence and does not know how the words composing it belong together? We all know boys who write utter bosh. They need to be taken right back to the beginnings which they are so hazy about.

It would be pleasant to find our learned teachers showing an interest in all this, and becoming alive to the individual manner of each pupil, watching him develop and seeing when he is ready for rational apprenticeship. There are works on the subject that are well worth reading. We dare not be complacent, with the young people trusting us as they do. If our purpose is more than to impart information, we must pause to consider the question of learning, because a boy's real progress in his studies will be his progress in the art of learning. Contemporary psychology gives it a lot of attention. It would be worth our while to discover what has been done.

Now another question arises: if the child advances by means of exercises done in a given subject, is it wise to expect the advance to be continued in a related subject, or in a completely different one?

It is an important question, after all. If the answer is in the negative, the training acquired through doing one set of exercises is practically confined to that one field. If the answer is in the affirmative, we are entitled to expect a general gain in training to be the result of a particular exercise. *A priori* we do not know which is right, experimental research alone will show, for by merely thinking it over we get precisely nowhere.

School children who have done hundreds of problems on *interest* are now better at answering questions on *interest*: but to what extent this has increased their capacity for dealing with other problems, we do not know. To take the matter a step further, how far can we claim that they have developed their intelligence to the point where it can now cope with totally different problems: abstract logic, for instance, or the elucidation of a difficult text, or moral judgment?

Research done does suggest that we need to be very prudent in airing opinions that are not based on the experimental method. When two boys of similar mental capacity reveal common elements, there is certainly common gain. But what of the contrary? And yet by the way teachers talk you would think there was no problem at all, but evident positive transference. We discuss training the mind, and talk over the studies likely to be conducive to this end: it is assuming too much on our part; like driving full tilt without check along a dangerous road. There are certain books and articles that put things in a wrong light, and we need to be distrustful of them. For though we are perfectly entitled to express an opinion, and to consider that the form of education we preconize is preferable, we have no right to declare it is the only valid one. In Arnould Clausse's view, civilization is "the material, moral and spiritual acquisition of a given historical environment, whereas culture is the reflective attitude of intelligent minds to the said acquisition". Our present-day civilization, consisting as it does of material factors and scientific progress, social administration, economics and politics, and moral, intellectual, æsthetic and religious realities, can be comprehended by the man of culture who is in a position to appreciate, understand, and measure it against the scale of values he recognizes.

In addition, the author holds that education consists primarily in a child's adaptation to his civilized environment: historically, this is not always a cultured one. "An opinion which is only the expression of a collective view, in which, consequently, there is no synthesis nor any personal appreciation, is an element of civilization, but it is not an element of culture." A readily acceptable teaching ideal would be one that equated civilization and culture.

But a great effort would be required: for an opinion to form about the facts of civilization, those facts must be thoroughly well known. Hence the temptation to make certain studies or certain exercises provide a training that could be termed "general", with the aim of producing a reflexive attitude in the intelligence towards all the problems and activities on which it was brought to bear. "General in an even wider sense too, because it would automatically be adequate to deal with every situation that might arise, and would acquire a universal validity, being always and everywhere appropriate. Here we have an easily grasped and alluring thesis, equally applicable to Neanderthal Man and a contemporary European."

"Thus conceived, mental life takes on an existence of its own, independent of the pull of environment. Teaching could then be deliberately remote from life, all contact with contingent reality being considered dangerous. And indeed the strength and virtue of the mind is that it is sovereign and absolute. It has first and foremost to safeguard its own integrity by safeguarding its universality. Its rôle will be mainly to apply the abstract and immutable norms of logic to changing, relative reality. Thus the 'mind' must be 'trained', and its security assured, together with the logical fatality of its operations. Forming the mind, and imparting information, will henceforth be irreconcilable opposites. Montaigne's famous dictum will be invoked, 'a well-made head rather than a full one'—sundered from its context (which points the meaning very differently). The view will no doubt prevail that 'culture is what is left when the rest has been forgotten. . . .'

"Skill in arousing interest will cease to have the slightest importance, naturally. Interest is but the manifestation of a tendency, and therefore always expresses a relation between the living creature and its environment; interest, indeed, is an enemy here, because, of its very essence, it is a link with life, that is, with the realities from which the pupil is to be systematically detached.

"Thus would evolve that curious theory of 'effort for its own sake', which is the negation of all biological science: on this theme the philosopher, Alain, in his day, produced a series of variations as specious as they are brilliant, to the loud applause of all the educational pundits."

It looks as though we have quite lost sight of the problem we were considering, that of the transference of a gain made through one particular exercise. Far from it. Here it is, as large as life: If you elect to put the child's mind out of touch with reality, and to "cultivate" it without regard to environment, it is doubtless because you are of the firm opinion that a child's intelligence lives a life of its own, with no need for nourishment; so that what was gained in mathematics is a gain to the mind as such; and a gain in parsing is a gain as such; you declare that positive transference has taken place as a result of those exercises, and you go on asserting that it is so, in spite of the psychologists' warnings and calls for prudence. But very elementary reflection, assisted by positive psychology, proves how necessary it is to re-examine the most sacred notions in this field.

It may seem odd that we have so far completely neglected the much-discussed new developments in education. For surely the whole system of teaching based on holding interest and creating centres of interest, and all the interconnected methods and syllabuses, is a product of modern psychology. Many writers on the subject say no less, and base their own views on this supposition. But the facts are otherwise.

The discoveries of child psychology gave rise to numerous theories of education; but not one of those so much in favour today is a necessary corollary to it. Modern educational theory is no more scientific than any other and needs divesting of all pretensions to be so; quite apart from the fact that it would be extremely difficult to pin it down and discover what exactly its present creed is; and no less difficult to say where it starts and what it includes. It is a real wilderness, which we will not attempt to penetrate. One very good reason for not doing so is that we find so little evidence in it of contemporary psychology, which is what we are here to discuss. That is not to say we should despise the new trends, there is even a good deal we can learn from them: but again, that is outside our subject.

VI. CONCLUSION

I only have one short conclusion to draw. We asked modern psychology what it could tell us of the relation of teacher and taught. Here is the answer, offered to the unbiased teacher for his consideration. He will see that modern psychology is not concerned with telling him what he ought to do, for that problem has a practical setting and science is only there to impart information. It is up to him, once he is better informed, to see whether he was on the wrong track or not. It is never too late to be honest and admit to a mistake. And it is never too late to start doing sounder and more effecttive educational work.

V

PSYCHOLOGY AND VOCATION

By Abbé Louis Évely

Principal of Cardinal Mercier College, Braine l'Alleud

PROPERLY speaking, a priest's vocation consists in a call from his bishop, and it is he who judges a candidate's aptitude, and the needs of the Christian community. But this call from authority is usually addressed to someone who has heard another call, a previous and inward one inviting him to dedicate his life to God. Thus the religious vocation, in its broader sense, precedes the vocation to the priesthood and normally presupposes it. In our time at least, a bishop chooses his priests from among those desiring to be consecrated to God who offer themselves to the Church and place themselves at its disposal.

These two vocations are distinct from one another: one, the religious vocation, is inward and independent, born of a personal response to a personal call from God. The other, the priestly vocation, is born of the call of ecclesiastical authority; it is outward and subordinate.

The separate nature of the two vocations might, indeed, become even more evident. A religious vocation, even when offered to the Church, is not necessarily a vocation to the priesthood. The bishop chooses among the candidates proposed and no one can claim the right to be selected. But it might conceivably happen that the Church would one day choose its priests not only from among those who offer themselves because of a religious vocation. The needs of the Christian community might cause the bishops to propose priesthood to men who had never thought of giving themselves to God in that particular way. Somewhat similar cases arose during the first centuries of our era. We can imagine the advantage it would be, in times of persecution for instance, to ordain devout bachelors or exemplary fathers of families. It would be a reversal of the present tendency to link the priesthood more and more closely to the religious vocation. The monastic orders are already tending to return to primitive practice by not ordaining all their monks to be priests; numbers of them hold that the priesthood is a special, different, vocation, binding to tasks and charges which they would find it difficult to reconcile with their state as religious.

Then the bishops would no longer impose the monastic way of life on all their priests, but would ordain them chiefly for the functions they were to perform in the Catholic community.

If a more pronounced difference between the religious life and the priestly life were to develop, it would have a variety of repercussions. It is obvious that one of the great reasons for the progress of the modern Church is the sanctification of the clergy, and this has come about largely through the increasing identification of the sacerdotal state and the religious state. The exercise of priestly functions requires holiness. The two forms of vocation could not be separated without creating a grave danger of regression in the Church. But it might happen that sacerdotal spirituality, which hitherto has too closely imitated the spirituality of the religious orders, would begin to affirm its own values: devotion, initiative, energy, responsibility—the ones that answer the requirements of the apostolate.

If we were only concerned with vocation to the priesthood, our present task would be an easy one. We should need to ask but one question: What are the aptitudes that make a candidate acceptable to his bishop? We should enumerate the intellectual qualities (knowledge, culture, judgment), the moral qualities (energy, detachment, piety), and physical qualities (integrity, bodily and mental health). We should refer to various books on medical obstacles to vocations. Of course the medical men do not give a verdict on the vocation itself, but only on its setting, describing the mental states that are irreconcilable with the religious life. Really clear-cut obstacles are very rare. The cases that come to our notice are usually only moderate ones, equally susceptible of aggravation or improvement, and the difficulty lies in estimating possible future developments. It all depends on how things are likely to go.

We should also compile a table of the candidates' various temperaments, and their capacity to answer the demands of diverse ecclesiastical functions. Mgr De Smedt went so far as to say that seminarists all looked alike: you could tell them by the shape of their heads.

But this is taking us right away from our real subject, which is not the orientation of vocations, but their detection. Judged on his physical and moral qualities, a candidate might seem admirably suitable for a priestly function or for the monastic life, without necessarily having a religious vocation at all. We do not believe that the possession of qualifications constitutes a vocation. And here precisely is our problem: When may a man legitimately conclude that he has a religious vocation? Because of the fact that nowadays every call to the priesthood is preceded by a religious vocation, to the extent that most people confuse the two, we may safely, and without neglecting our theme, devote our attention primarily to the psychology of the latter.

The religious vocation is manifest in our desire to give ourselves wholly to God, and this humble, deep desire, persistent and trial-proof, is for us Christians more powerful than any purely natural force. It comes of a grace, a free act of God, and that is why we see it as a call, a vocation. The Council of Trent declared that without the inspiration and help of the Holy Spirit no one can make a true act of faith, hope, charity, or repentance. How much more of an inspired act of profound charity and a response to a stirring of grace, is the one whereby a man offers himself to God for the whole of his life. So to our mind a vocation does not consist in a call that is felt or heard, nor in an act of generosity, nor in a movement of devotion or renunciation, but in supernatural grace which may adopt any of those channels or not do so at all; which may speak distinctly or confusedly; and may be manifest through an attraction as—even at one and the same time—through a revulsion. The recognition of this grace is the whole and sole recognition of vocation. God's action on a soul, in itself mysterious and beyond our understanding, is registered in certain effects, and it is there we must learn to read it. This reading requires a skill which early spiritual writers codified in their rules for the recognition of spirits.

The recognition of a religious vocation is more complex nowadays, since the discovery of the potential wealth of conjugal spirituality. Formerly, marriage was all too often presented as a makeshift solution for men resigned to spiritual mediocrity. Today theologians have demonstrated that marriage also leads to God and is a means of sanctification. Some of the best Christians have such an exalted and holy ideal of marriage that it becomes a sort of religious vocation. Instead of distinguishing, as formerly, between a religious vocation and marriage, we now have to recognize three distinct states: celibacy for the man who lacks the courage, generosity or perseverance to found and maintain a home, and would find the burden too heavy; a religious vocation in the broader sense, for the man seeking a companion with whom to spend his life in mutual emulation in self-sacrifice, devotion and spiritual growth; and the religious vocation proper for the man who gives himself entirely and directly to God, to belong to Him exclusively.

In some minds, even some of the best, this distinction becomes blurred. Here is a passage from an article by Fr Chevignard giving an account of a study-week held for novice-mistresses, entitled *Recognizing a Vocation*: "It seems to me that we may humbly infer God's call in a soul when we perceive it to have a steady desire to belong totally, humbly, exclusively, to God, to Christ and His service. And we should add, in the normal course this desire is accompanied by peace and joy." Fr Chevignard then remarks that "exclusive" is the specific term. He recognizes, however, that the desire to belong to God alone is true in a way for all Christians. But, he adds, "The detachment required of a woman in the home is merely interior; in the religious, it is effective". Now it seems to us that the more important form of detachment is precisely the one that the writer deprecates, calling it "merely interior". A widow, for instance, does not become a nun simply because her detachment has become "effective". In these circumstances, the religious vocation is separated from marriage by a hair's breadth only: an interior detachment, exteriorized or not exteriorized. However theologians split this hair, the majority of Christians wonder if the difference is really such as to justify all the praises lavished on the religious state for its higher status.

Modern men and women have also read of the psychological discoveries and acquired a certain fear of complexes and repressions. They desire human expansion and fulfilment. They see in the religious life a source of emotional disequilibrium and the risk of compensation in vice: for who can be sure of properly sublimating his instincts?

The dignity of marriage is further enhanced by the fact that admission to it is a sacrament, which, let us admit the paradox, is not the case in religious dedication, so much more in need of graces, or so one would have thought. Canon Leclercq, in his rôle of *enfant terrible*, once wrote that "God intervenes in marriage in a more direct way and more categorically, than in a religious profession."

So now our boys and girls no longer have to choose between a religious vocation and marriage, the latter considered as the easy way to obtain the satisfaction of human instincts; but between two ways of perfection, two vocations to sanctity, and both are attractive to our young people, nearly all of them, from one point of view or another. Here is an example of what goes on in their minds: "Although it seems that every fibre in your being longs for marriage, because it is the realization of that divine, magic, moving thing, love; because it is a mutual giving, a striving hand in hand towards a common goal; because it is union, total trust, sustenance, life, joy; and also—though less clearly admitted—because marriage means something delightful and easy: yet, though everything in you cries out for marriage, there are also those odd incessant little calls to religion; what do they mean, I wonder; and the feelings and forebodings of being 'intended', when reading or talking of vocation and generosity and total self-surrender. Is it really a choice between making God the centre of your life, and marriage? If I were to marry, I should want to love God as much as I possibly could. On the other hand, are all those pinpricks from God the sign of a vocation, or not? Can God call someone to the religious life who does not want that life? Does the call not consist in the desire for it? It seems to me that if I said, I will dedicate myself to God, I should have no more liking for anything. Whereas if I were sure that I am made to love God in marriage, I should welcome God so much more warmly."

We may well wonder how the two vocations are best to be differentiated, and how a modern boy or girl is to be helped to understand whether the call is to serve God in marriage or in religious celibacy.

Every Christian is called to perfection. A desire for holiness is not a sufficient criterion for a religious vocation. The laity have to strive for holiness with the same vigour as the priest. It is all the faithful whom the Master commands to be perfect, whose life in the world is to be like Christ's, as St John says, "Our life in the world should be like his" (1 John iv. 17); and of whom St Peter dares to write, "You are a chosen race, a royal priesthood, a consecrated nation, a people God means to have for himself; it is yours to proclaim the exploits of the God who has called you out of darkness into his marvellous light" (1 Peter ii. 9).

The difference between the laity and the religious is not a different end in view, but different means to attain it. We are all basically called to the same vocation, and the proof is that in heaven we shall all be alike (at the resurrection of the dead husbands will have no wives nor a wife a husband) and we shall all meet at the same goal, and all be completely happy in heaven, in the happiness of Another. We shall be so closely identified with this Other One through love and self-renunciation, that the happiness of the Other will enter into us and give us full contentment.

To reach that state, two ways lie open to us.

For some, God is so real a Being, so alive, so near, that He counts for more than anything in the world. God in the majesty of His liturgy, God in the poverty of His poor, God in the faithfulness of their faith, seems to them the one great reality of the whole universe. They work better when they are working for Him; they are happier when they are nearest to Him; they understand more readily when He is spoken of. They live from God and for God, immediately and without intermediary. And in this life they already begin that great liturgy, that vast theocentric activity, which is our

eternal vocation. Their joy is to go to God directly and to
God alone.

On the other hand, there are others who believe in God,
love Him and revere Him. But to some extent as an abstraction. They do not try to live from Him alone. To draw them
out of their inertia, or distract them from their egoism, a
human motive has to enter into play. They will do good if
there is a human interest in doing so; running the show,
seeing more of a dear friend, making a handsome profit.
Doubtless it is all done for God in the long run, but God is
not the motive, He is not what nourishes their effort and
finally rewards it; He is only its ultimate justification. So they
need to find some human support in life to encourage them
to do the good of which they are capable. If they only had
God to sustain them, they might be less good, less active, less
generous than they will be when responsible for a family or
a business. And it is precisely the exertions required of them
in that state of life which will lead them, progressively purified, to a perfection of which they were at first incapable. A
man in love learns to come out of his shell and take an interest
in someone else, and this leads to a yet wider range of interest.
The joy of loving gradually quietens down and deepens. The
demands of faithful love now emerge and draw from him
a generosity and unselfishness that go from strength to
strength. Soon, acting generously will come as a matter of
course, for the sake of the happiness given rather than personal
satisfaction. He comes to love wife and children for their own
sakes, not possessively, admitting his children's right to go
out and live their own lives. On the day he must leave them
and die, his heart is ready to hand them over trustingly to a
more powerful one than himself. He learnt to love the good
of others, and was then initiated into love of Good for its own
sake. Love was his education in charity. Indeed, in every
human vocation Jesus' prophecy to St Peter finds fulfilment:

"As a young man thou wouldst gird thyself and walk where thou hadst the will to go, but when thou hast grown old, another shall gird thee, and carry thee where thou goest, not of thy own will" (John xxi. 18).

So the difference between religious vocation and marriage is not a matter of interior detachment and exterior detachment (both detachments must be interior, and if they are not truly so, exterior detachment is of little use); nor is it a matter of detachment proposed and detachment achieved (for both accept the proposed detachment, and neither is completely successful in achieving it); it is, rather, a difference in the means used: for a husband, marriage is the human means of detachment, an education in perfect charity. For a religious, God is immediately and persistently the reason and the means of all his efforts in detachment.

Here we disagree with Canon Leclercq, who says that the aim of marriage is, normally, happiness, thus distinguishing it by a hint of egoism, while admitting that for certain picked couples the aim of marriage is an ideal of perfection. Couples with that end in view, who have not yet embarked on their marriage, are of special interest to us, since they are the ones we have to advise. The rest will not come to us in any case.

The outstanding characteristic of the religious vocation is a very lively sense of God. It is born of an encounter with the living God. To a religious, God is manifest as the most important, most present, most active, most loving of all beings. The manifestation varies according to individuals and ages. The Absolute reaches us by a multitude of channels.

In childhood, a perception of the supernatural is so lively, faith is so spontaneous and natural, that most children brought up in truly Christian families have a religious vocation at the age of ten.

Adolescence comes as a disturbance, blunting the call of

God, but it generally reappears in another form: a desire to
be generous, an ambition to remain wholly at the disposal
of the great causes that exact a man's all, unencumbered by
family or impediment of any kind. And at last, but generally
a good deal later, many feel called to the priesthood on seeing
man and the world as it is. During a war, or in a factory, or in
their family, or simply through someone they love, they have
a revelation of the incredible depth of human wretchedness
and frailty. They realize they will never be able to remedy this
wretchedness merely by becoming a doctor or a mining
engineer or a lawyer or a business man, and that it is vain to
try to help mankind by offering merely bread, coal, or health
of body. They have come across a few generous souls doing
real work, and feel they must not be left to do it alone. They
reach the point when they could not bear to spend their time
and energies on themselves, their families, their business, and
they enter the harvest field because the harvest is so abundant
and the workers are so few.

Naturally, this call always has its share of illusions. In
youth there is a tendency to want to use God rather than
serve God. But every great human enterprise begins with a
halo of illusions. The essential thing is to be sure the core is
sound. People enter marriage supposedly to enjoy happiness,
and what they learn is chiefly self-sacrifice. But there was
never an intention of excluding this. You enter the seminary
to convert the world and you learn, sometimes very much
later, that it would be a wonderful thing to be able to convert
yourself, so that God might be known and loved and glorified
in at least one soul consecrated to Him. And you discover that
it is really what you wanted all the time, though you were
incapable of saying it in so many words when you first tried
to interpret your vocation.

The authentic part of every vocation is the active presence,
the living love of God, perceived, taking possession, and

gradually predominating. That is the sure sign of vocation. Even if other ideals, like self-sacrifice, education or social work, may seem uppermost in a candidate's mind, or at least in his attempt to express it, a genuine religious vocation is present only if, very deep within him, these good works interest him because they are from God, and have no meaning apart from Him.

Coventry Patmore tells somewhere of what first gave a religious turn to his thoughts: it was an idea that cropped up in his mind, of how fine and splendid a thing it would be, did a God exist with whom one could entertain a relation of love and obedience. A religious is someone for whom, by the grace of God, such a relation has become real, he is someone who can make it his life, breath and nourishment. To be a religious is to find peace, plenitude, satisfaction in God, in solitary prayer, and in services rendered to others for love of God. "An outcast among my own brethren, a stranger to my own mother's children, always I can keep the Lord within sight; always he is at my right hand, to make me stand firm. As for me, I will come with upright heart into thy presence innocent; and when thy glory dawns, I shall be well content."

That this way, and not marriage, is the better way is clear; the reason is, its simplicity; it makes eternal life begin at once, it consecrates us to God in end and means. Of course every Christian gives himself to God, and marriage is one way of doing it. But so many become bogged in the means they choose. To go to God via marriage is to go the longer way round. Such loops are valuable for most people, who would lose heart on the steep climb up, but no one ought deliberately to choose roundabout ways.

To summarize: a call to the religious vocation may or may not be ratified by ecclesiastical authority, but its authenticity does not depend on the authentification. It is however otherwise for the vocation to the priesthood, which is essentially conditioned by the bishop's call, no one having the right to it before being called by the bishop.

Finally, a psychological distinction needs to be made between the pure religious vocation and the vocation to the priesthood; or rather, to keep our initial distinction in view, between the religious vocation as such and the religious vocation placed at the disposal of the Church. To my mind, the latter is characterized by the functions and charges it accepts. Everyone has his own plan for saving the world, and many are ready to fight and destroy the world in their effort to impose their panacea. A candidate for the priesthood, however, knows that the world is already saved, he knows that Someone has loved and saved the world and believes it is sufficient to adopt the means He instituted, in all faith and humility going on effecting the Redemption He wrought. To offer yourself to the bishop's selection is to accept to save the world by the Mass, the sacraments, and the preaching of Jesus. Indeed, this commitment is, as observation shows, part of every vocation, whether initially due to admiration for a priest one would like to resemble, or love of the liturgy, or pity for the masses with no shepherd. But the more we become priests, the more we are conscious of what our vocation is, and the more, is it not true, we gain confidence in the supernatural means whose efficacy is, happily, independent of our worthiness; and the more we learn to believe in and submit to a plan of salvation which infinitely surpasses our ideas and our experience.

VI

PSYCHOLOGY AND PRAYER

By Canon Désiré Joos
Director of Charities, Diocese of Tournai

I

HERE "prayer" shall be taken as meaning "life". According to Alexis Carrel in his essay on Prayer, it is "the raising of the *soul* to God. As an act of love and adoration to Him, the donor of that marvel, life. Indeed prayer represents man's effort to *communicate* with an invisible Being, Creator of all that is, sovereign Wisdom, Power and Beauty, Father and Saviour of each one of us. It does not consist in the mere recitation of formulas, far from it: true prayer represents a mystical *state* in which the mind is absorbed in God. This state is not of an intellectual nature." Anyhow it is not purely intellectual. There is that profound life of the soul that lies on the far side of discursive meditation and vocal prayer, when the soul is wholly united to God by what is most essential to it: mind and will, loving intelligence. In prayer man gives himself entire and is given entire by what he is at his greatest depth. And this state underlies discursive meditation, vocal prayer and ritual.

Another point to clarify is important in these days of existentialism: prayer is far from being a sort of "sublimation", liberation and perfect control of the Ego, diverse and dispersed as it is; prayer exists as life with what is not the Ego, life with God, the Father God whom simple people approach so naturally with neither formulas nor methods of prayer.

It is He who produces *unity* in a man who prays. God, "that Absolute", as Fr Maréchal describes Him, "Being pure and simple, Being *above all determination*, who is at once latent motive force, ideal form of unity, and ultimate goal of all the strivings of the human soul: at the term of them all, at their point of convergence—possibly inaccessible—where the One and the Good merge in intuition of Being; for only in this intuition, at the extreme limit of the created spirit's capacity, may the soul in a moment achieve the supreme unity of speculative thought and the unadulterated possession of love."

It would not matter if no philosopher had described this "becoming" of the soul which is unification in God: we have but to turn to St John to rediscover the marvel of grace within us that is prayer: a coming of God into us, so that we may be "one with Him"; culminating in an awareness and loving intending of the divine intentions in a state of loving faith.

But God consummates this union only in the man who is free. There must be an acceptance and a welcome, and liberation from all "determinisms", for this mysterious, ineffable union to be accomplished.

The praying soul is only praying if it is free, and unity occurs from above downwards. How well we know it when, after a period of experimentation we turn, distrustful of technical aids, to prayer. It is interesting to observe how lay people who never went through the mill of a seminary or novitiate are often more prompt than we are to grasp prayer as a live emergence of the soul and not the product of a system. Joseph Folliet, for one, deprecates the modern tendency to work out "techniques of interiority" to achieve spiritual life. Many concrete cases could doubtless be cited, showing up our timidity before men, our distrust before God, due to our habit of giving priority to methodical rules which,

we claim, shall "unify the soul and assure us of divine concurrence". This is a good point to reflect upon, for some of
the methods currently used in dialogue Mass, for instance, as
well as other forms of worship, need radical revision. Yet in
certain cases prayer seems so well able to prevail and soar above
the dominant preoccupations of the psyche.

Are young people more sensitive to prayer than we are?
The discontinuity in them between a free, loving spirit and
lower functions and sensations may have less unfortunate
consequences in them than in us. At any rate young people
who are encouraged to pray, having learnt who God is—
God, the Creator and Father, in all the beauty and depth of
the appellation, as revealed by the incarnate Son—sometimes
leave us dumbfounded at what they reach in prayer. No
elaborate psychology course was needed, everything was
resolved as it were from above; of course it would be hard to
determine what was due to grace and what to nature, but
the facts speak for themselves.

I have in mind a girl, gravely ill, slowly dying in terrible
pain. The doctors thought it necessary to administer large
doses of calming drugs. As soon as the medicine took effect,
cutting out the use of reason and will, the child began to
moan and went on doing so till she gradually fell asleep.
On waking, the moaning started again, but when pain
once more became conscious, the mind took control. She
managed to smile, it was a very brave act, and she was
praying quietly all the time, committing herself to God
amazingly.

That is an example of the predominating and profound
influence of prayer: today we hear all too often how man is
enmeshed in the subconscious and a slave of instinct, and
freedom is supposed to be a delusion.

The influence of the *time* given to prayer is worth noting.
Prolonged prayer gives freedom full play because its activity

continues while the inferior faculties capitulate to the passing minutes. Indeed various experiments only endorse the assumption that length of time has a pretty considerable influence on quality of prayer. Holy Year exercises carried out by students, long sessions in church observed in the case of people of no remarkable culture, indicate that the longer prayer lasts, the more concentration is helped at a given moment; the less one is concerned with oneself, the more prayer strips one bare; and the greater the influence it has on life and on other prayers.

If there is any one phenomenon of liberation, it is prayer. Prayer first as the fruit of grace but also of deliberate effort. Prayer is so different from exaltation of the ego or a state of passive low pressure: it is the fine point of effort and the mystery of grace, and consists in nothing but awareness of union with the loved one, in peace and calm at its own level, though the surface of the mind may be in turmoil. St Paul of the Cross called this state "peripheral" and distractions he called "buzzing flies". And Claudel relates how, "for many years, O my God, every day at five o'clock in the afternoon I have been the suppliant of your blessed Cross . . .". Most of the time nothing happens, or nothing perceptible. And a man can count himself happy if after a long period of constantly renewed lying-in-wait (nothing anthropocentric about this: only a God and a soul; no psychological machinery) he finds that in the depths of him something is occurring about as noticeable as the crumbling away of a grain of sand. (Prayer is not something wrought on me by myself, not something that can be felt, or scarcely at all.) "But is it nothing, purely and simply to exist? Is it nothing to *co-exist* with that lamp, that tiny speck of red light, pitched now higher, now suddenly lower, that over in the sanctuary suffers God. (The flame of the lamp is the symbol of the presence of God suffering, in whom praying man communicates.) The Passion is now Patience. It is You, Yourself, O my God, it is the Cross. Indeed, I know it is You."

Although he uses different terminology, Pierre Guérin says much the same thing: "Prayer is a sort of startled and desperate leap into the blue to reach another world in which the conscious mind no longer feels itself a prisoner because it is no longer product but principle. What gives objectivity to the attempt is the otherness of what is aspired to." "In prayer is found pure spirituality which delivers us from the world; we try to escape from the necessities of matter by means of a fourth dimension which is the life of the spirit; and once within in, *though still subject to the material conditions of life*, we are no longer weighed down by them, being like a prisoner set free from captivity, not by leaping over the walls of his prison but by intensifying his inner life till he no longer feels his chains."

At least it is now clear why we were anxious to avoid a certain terminology which makes of prayer a means, a remedy for the ills of body and soul. As the highest expression of love, prayer is the highest expression of life: it is the very heart of freedom; it is liberation of man by God: our discomforts and lack of focus, our instincts and our unconscious, will be subordinated and disciplined—or at least they will not be continuous with our prayer.

II

If the soul is a praying soul to the extent that it is free, its freedom is affected and limited by a good many other factors. Much attention has already been given to the subject of the mysterious union of body and spirit, nature and grace, and we have nothing new to add. To reaffirm the transcendence and immanence of God's Spirit and grace is still not to define God's plumbing of a soul at prayer. We cannot do it. But every day we have it painfully brought home to us how perceptible the influence of biological and physiological factors on our prayer still is.

As Fr Olphe-Galliard, s.j., says, we have to admit that here as elsewhere God does not eliminate nature.

But prayer is something so wonderful, and God's intervention so special, that, as he notes with circumspection, spiritual writers do counsel methods, elucidated and improved in the light of psychological discovery, without professing for them "an absolute, blind cult", and presenting them "not rigidly but with elbow-room".

Thus cautioned, let us now approach the confused and diversified world of the lower regions of the soul, where the pure upward surge of its peaks is rooted in a particular manner. Let us admit at once that if there is no common measure between the two worlds, there is that mysterious capacity for union: all the powers of the soul, even the most obscure, are an "increasing approximation to the higher faculties"—to quote a phrase of Maréchal's from another context.

This way of understanding the unity of the soul is the one taught by modern psychologists like De Greeff, who says, "There exists in man, anterior to all experience, a certain number of dispositions to act which form a basic reserve of energy"; and he goes on to say that without this reserve the higher life is an impossibility: "We declare that instinct is at the beginning of all psychic life, and that where there is no store of basic, instinctive energies, no reserve of urges and desires—no mysterious reserve of mysterious energy—there can be no growth and blossoming forth of a higher life in a human soul". Consequently we do well to recognize that a connection does exist between the higher and lower life of our soul. We observe that the psychologists mentioned describe their union as an overlapping and not as the outcome of a deadly struggle. So it is an error to try to situate our inner conflict there: moral effort has its place in the growth and blossoming of the instincts towards unity of soul.

There is an extraordinary diversity of instincts and deeper urges. Individuals differ, and the key-note that strikes from the depth of every soul, and accounts for it, has a very different ring in different people. Although one man may be rather like another, he is *essentially* different. We conclude that if we want to deal fairly with him and show him how to pray, we must first get to know our man, and only then try to direct his prayer in the way it should go. Prayer is very personal, and because of the mobility of our feelings it is one thing today and tomorrow another.

Prayer is a *personal* problem. If an example is needed, here it is: how many of us have the courage to hold a book of meditations open in our hands for any length of time, or with any sense of profit? These prayers belong to someone else who wants me to use them. Why? Well, precisely because of their otherness, and what they can tell me about God. Apart from that, they are but someone else's prayers, the complex that is someone else, and nothing is more wearisome than trying to make another man's experience our own.

Prayer must be our *own* prayer. Life is constantly modifying my ego, bringing in its train such things as indigestion, an atonal condition, a neurasthenic tendency. But the prayer of a neurasthenic is prayer, far more so than the prayer of a healthy man said, or prayed, by a neurasthenic. Nor is it wise to propose to the laity modes of prayer that are specifically meant for men or women religious.

We could all cite cases similar to the following. A young man was unable to pray because his aural imagination completely absorbed him: a Bach fugue haunted him all through prayer-time. It was suggested that he compose religious

9*

melodies during his prayer-time and put words to them, singing them interiorly. That young man's prayer was saved. A girl was distressed at not being able to get rid of inconsequential dreams in her prayers; various kinds of substitution were proposed, but she was not freed from her difficulty till the doctor discovered that she was backward in certain respects; things were simplified for her and she was helped to learn to pray like a child.

Wherever there is a problem of the personality there is also a problem of prayer. We must know ourself, if it is ourself; and know others, if it is others. Temperamental, biological and hereditary diversity has to be allowed for. Needless to say, really difficult cases must be referred to a specialist— priest or doctor according to the nature of the trouble.

III

To everyone the accomplishment of his own unity and the use of his own powers. We agree, it is a personal question. But at the same time it is universal and general rules do exist.

The body and its needs, the instincts, all the functions of the mind are there for all and sundry, requiring to be nourished and contented so that they may cease protesting and dispersing a soul seeking its unity.

Repose may do it: a quiet poise of the body, composure of the lower functions that percolate into the antechambers of prayer; the senses may be appealed to, the affections focused, the emotions attuned to the present object of prayer, interest may be roused, and—if need be—thoughts may be guided.

Thus all functions are directed towards one and the same object. They become alert on going into action; and all, from the somatic to thought itself, "will foster the flowering of inward devotion" (Maréchal).

Suddenly we see the point of rites, liturgical gestures, spoken words, pictures, and asceticism itself, and their true value as a means of training our inferior movements towards unity. As Fr Maréchal says, "All contribute to the unity of the spiritual life".

I wonder if we make sufficient use of the Gospel. It is so inherently universal, yet it impinges on the world of the senses with inexpressible sureness and delicacy of touch. Take the exhortation to trust our heavenly Father implicitly (Matthew vi. 25-34): This can wholly captivate a man, placing him in the very presence of the God of all goodness and compelling him in some sort to grasp God's transcendence. Note the appeal to eyes and ears: there are flowers in the fields, birds being fed; the imagination is fired; personal interest is aroused; a touch of glory lights up all the corners of the soul, and there emerges the evidence of self peeled off and stripped away, that holds us spellbound. Step by step we are led on; every step is much more than a reflex action: the impetus is stronger and the effects more far-reaching.

IV

So far we have spoken of man alone, a man praying. But we may not isolate him from his environment, and psychology does not do so. Environment has a great influence on the functions of the soul. This is not the place to describe the effects of the outside world on prayer. But diet is important for the organism and the psyche, especially during growth. Poor digestion has a bad effect on prayer. Climate, too, counts; excessive heat or cold reduces our activity. November and March are months of greatest productivity. There is the family circle to consider and the changes that occur in it (bereavement, separation, divorce . . .): all this can profoundly modify the psyche, releasing or stemming the desire to pray. A lesser influence in psychologists' eyes, but not negligible by any means, is that of school and career. Why not study the prayer of a nurse, or a miner, or a tradesman, for instance? There is the influence of social contacts to take into account, and the events and occupations that fill our lives.

It is certain that all these factors colour our prayer, but, we repeat, without determining it. In the degree to which they are discerningly *directed* towards unity of soul, they even cease to be a menace, or a burden, or an element destructive of equilibrium in any way.

We should be inclined to give the name of "recollection" to the unifying disposition of the soul, i.e. serene attention to the end in view united to strength of mind in resisting distraction. Is not this the direct way to spiritual equilibrium? In prayer we gain inward peace and calm. The psychologists endorse this: we gain physical and mental equilibrium in a sense, and chiefly, equilibrium of action—which we believe prayer alone can effect; moral equilibrium too: all due to prayer.

"Among people where praying is customary", said Carrel, "there is greater persistence of the sense of duty and responsibility, less jealousy and wickedness, some kindness to others. We may take it as proven that, with parity of intellect, character and moral worth are of a higher standard among people who pray, even if only badly, than among people who do not pray."

v

Willy-nilly, this unification of life can take place only gradually. Spiritual writers bemoan it; psychologists talk of the "becoming" of the soul. At times, the mind gives up trying and now and again the lower functions gain the upper hand. Lifting up the soul to God, ritual gesture, devotional practices may all grow mechanical and fall to the level of reflexes. Fr Maréchal is still optimistic even here, allowing us to believe that even at the lower level there is "orientation towards the spirit". A sustained effort does not of itself produce definite orientations; it may become easier by dint of sheer perseverance, but it is still not certain to bring a man unity.

What theology teaches is prudence; reminding us that unity comes from God, and that a subtle self-reliance sometimes brings about the worst downfalls. A soul can feel so free in regard to sin, even after long and fierce spiritual struggles. The mystery of freedom is beyond our ken and beyond the psychologists' too. There are moments when God alone holds us to Him. But an attempt at constructive action can be made, within the bounds of our time and space, though it is at best precarious, and we have to work away at it patiently. But trustfully too: such is our lot, as Christians.

LIST OF BOOKS REFERRED TO

CHAPTER I

CURRAN, A., *Counselling in Catholic Life and Education*, New York, Macmillan, 1952. Preface by Cardinal Tisserand.

NUTTIN, CANON JOSEPH, *Psychanalyse et conception spiritualiste de l'homme*, Louvain, Publications universitaires, 1951.

—— "Séminaire et équilibre psychique" in *Le Cardinal Mercier, fondateur de séminaire*, Louvain, Séminaire Léon XIII, 1951.

CHAPTER II

RICŒUR, P., *Philosophie de la volonté*, Vol. 1: *Le volontaire et l'involontaire*, Paris, 1950.

RIMAUD, REV. J., "Les psychologues contre la morale", *Études*, Oct. 1949.

CHAPTER III

ARTHUS, Dr, *Un monde inconnu: nos enfants*, Tournai and Paris, Casterman, 1951.

BARUK, DR, *Psychiatrie médicale, physiologique et expérimentale*, Paris, Spes, 1948.

—— *Précis de psychiatrie*, Paris, Masson, 1950.

—— *Psychiatrie morale expérimentale, individuelle, et sociale*, Paris, Presses universitaires, 1950.

—— *Les méthodes scientifiques d'étude de la conscience morale en psychologie et psychopathologie*, Paris, Spes, 1951.

BERGE, DR A., "Le sentiment de la culpabilité chez l'enfant" in *Le coupable est-il un malade ou un pécheur?* Paris, Spes, 1950.

—— *L'éducation sexuelle et effective*, Paris, Editions du Scarabée, 1951.

BEIRNAERT, FR, S.J., "La sainteté dépend-elle du psychisme?" in *Études*, July-Aug. 1950.

BIOT, DR R., *Offensives biologiques contre la personne*, Paris, Spes, 1951.

COSSA, DR P., article in *Troubles et lumières*, Études Carmelitains, Paris, Desclée de Brouwer, 1949.

DALBIEZ, R., *La méthode psychoanalytique et la doctrine freudienne*, 2 vols., Paris, Desclée de Brouwer, 1949.

DALTO, DR A., "Comment on crée chez l'enfant une fausse culpabilité" in *Troubles et lumières*, Études Carmélitaines, Desclée de Brouwer, Paris, 1949.

GREEFF, DR E. DE, *L'homme et le péché*, Paris, Plon, 1938.

—— *Nos enfants et nous*, Tournai and Paris, Casterman, 1948.

HESNARD, DR A., *L'univers morbide de la faute*, Paris, 1949.

—— *Traité de sexologie normale et pathologique*, Paris, Payot, 1933.

KLUG, I., *Les profondeurs de l'âme*, Mulhouse, Salvator, 1939.

LEROUX, MGR E., article on "Scruples" in *La revue ecclésiastique de Liège*, Vols. 7 and 8.

LE MOAL, DR P., "Le psychiatre devant l'homosexuel" in *Les états intersexuels*, Paris, Lethielleux, 1950.

MOELLER, C., *Sagesse grecque et paradoxe chrétien*, Tournai, Casterman, 1948.

MOUNIER, E., *Traité du caractère*, Paris, Editions du Seuil, 1949.

NUTTIN, CANON JOSEPH, *Psychanalyse et conception spiritualiste de l'homme*, Louvain, 1951.

ODIER, DR C., *Les deux sources, consciente et inconsciente, de la vie morale*, Neuchâtel, Editions de la Baconnière, 1947.

TOURNIER, DR P., *De la solitude à la Communauté*, Neuchâtel, Delachaux et Niestlé.

—— *Médicine de la personne, ibid.*

—— *Technique et Foi, ibid.*

WEILL, SIMONE, *Intuitions préchrétiennes*, Paris, La Colombe, 1951.

CHAPTER IV

CLAUSSE, ARNOULD, *Introduction à l'histoire de l'éducation*, Brussels, De Boeck, 1951.

PIÉRON, H., *Psychologie différentielle*, Paris, 1949.

CHAPTER VI

CARREL, ALEXIS, *La Prière*, Paris, Éditions Universitaires; English trans. by D. de Ste Croix Wright, Hodder & Stoughton, 1947.

CLAUDEL, PAUL, *Un poète regarde la croix*, Paris, Gallimard.

FOLLIET, J., *L'avènement de Prométhée*, Paris, Chronique sociale de France, 1950.

GREEFF, DR E. DE, *Notre destinée et nos instincts*.

GUÉRIN, P., *Pensée constructive et réalités spirituelles*, Paris, Alcan, n.d.

MARÉCHAL, J., S.J., *Études sur la psychologie des mystiques*, 1924.

OLPHE-GALLIARD, M., S.J., *Technique et Contemplation*, Études Carmélitaines, Paris, 1949.

PAYOT, JULES, *L'éducation de la volonté*, 1941.

VERDUN, M., *Le caractère et ses corrélations*, Vol. 1: *Caractère, milieu, constitution*, Paris, Baillière, n.d.

WEATHERHEAD, LESLIE D., *Psychology in the Service of the Soul*, London.